THE

WORKS

OF

SOAME JENYNS

THE
WORKS

O F

SOAME JENYNS, Esq.

IN FOUR VOLUMES.

INCLUDING SEVERAL PIECES
NEVER BEFORE PUBLISHED,

TO WHICH ARE PREFIXED,

SHORT SKETCHES OF THE HISTORY OF
THE AUTHOR'S FAMILY,

AND ALSO OF HIS LIFE;

BY CHARLES NALSON COLE, Esq.

VOL. IV.

LONDON:
PRINTED FOR T. CADELL, IN THE STRAND.
M.DCC.XC.

Complete set - S.B.N. - 0.576.02103.2
This volume - S.B.N. - 0.576.02972.6

Republished in 1969 by Gregg International Publishers Limited
Westmead, Farnborough, Hants., England

Printed in Israel

A

V I E W

OF THE

INTERNAL EVIDENCE

OF THE

CHRISTIAN RELIGION.

Almost thou persuadest me to be a Christian.
Acts xxvi. 28.

A

V I E W, &c.

MOST of the writers, who have undertaken to prove the divine origin of the Christian Religion, have had recourse to arguments drawn from these three heads: the prophecies still extant in the Old Testament—the miracles recorded in the New—or, the internal evidence arising from that excellence, and those clear marks of supernatural interposition, which are so conspicuous in the religion itself. The two former have been sufficiently explained and enforced by the ablest pens; but the last, which seems to carry with it the greatest degree of conviction, has never, I think, been considered with that attention, which it deserves.

I mean not here to depreciate the proofs arising from either prophecies, or miracles: they both have, or ought to have, their pro-

per

per weight; prophecies are permanent miracles, whose authority is sufficiently confirmed by their completion, and are therefore solid proofs of the supernatural origin
of a religion, whose truth they were intended
to testify; such are those to be found in various parts of the scriptures relative to the
coming of the Messiah, the destruction of
Jerusalem, and the unexampled state in
which the Jews have ever since continued,
all so circumstantially descriptive of the
events, that they seem rather histories of past,
than predictions of future transactions; and
whoever will seriously consider the immense
distance of time between some of them and
the events which they foretell, the uninterrupted chain by which they are connected
for many thousand years, how exactly they
correspond with those events, and how totally unapplicable they are to all others in
the history of mankind; I say, whoever con-
siders these circumstances, he will scarcely
be persuaded to believe that they can be the
productions of preceding artifice, or poste-
rior

rior application, or can entertain the leaſt doubt of their being derived from ſupernatural inſpiration.

The miracles recorded in the New Teſtament to have been performed by Chriſt and his Apoſtles, were certainly convincing proofs of their divine commiſſion to thoſe who ſaw them; and as they were ſeen by ſuch numbers, and are as well atteſted, as other hiſtorical facts, and above all, as they were wrought on ſo great and ſo wonderful an occaſion, they muſt ſtill be admitted as evidence of no inconſiderable force; but, I think, they muſt now depend for much of their credibility on the truth of that religion, whoſe credibility they were at firſt intended to ſupport. To prove therefore the truth of the Chriſtian Religion, we ſhould begin by ſhewing the internal marks of divinity, which are ſtamped upon it; becauſe on this the credibility of the prophecies and miracles in a great meaſure depends: for if we have once reaſon to be convinced, that this religion is derived from a ſuperna-

B 3
tural

tural origin, prophecies and miracles will become so far from being incredible, that it will be highly probable, that a supernatural revelation should be foretold, and enforced by supernatural means.

What pure Christianity is, divested of all its ornaments, appendages, and corruption, I pretend not to say; but what it is not, I will venture to affirm, which is, that it is not the offspring of fraud or fiction: such, on a superficial view, I know it must appear to every man of good sense, whose sense has been altogether employed on other subjects; but if any one will give himself the trouble to examine it with accuracy and candor, he will plainly see, that however fraud and fiction may have grown up with it, yet it never could have been grafted on the same stock, nor planted by the same hand.

To ascertain the true system, and genuine doctrines of this religion, after the undecided controversies of above seventeen centuries, and to remove all the rubbish, which artifice and ignorance have been heaping upon it during

during all that time, would indeed be an arduous task, which I shall by no means undertake; but to shew, that it cannot possibly be derived from human wisdom, or human imposture, is a work, I think, attended with no great difficulty, and requiring no extraordinary abilities, and therefore I shall attempt that, and that alone, by stating, and then explaining the following plain and undeniable propositions.

First, That there is now extant a book intitled the New Testament.

Secondly, That from this book may be extracted a system of religion intirely new, both with regard to the object and the doctrines, not only infinitely superior to, but unlike every thing, which had ever before entered into the mind of man.

Thirdly, That from this book may likewise be collected a system of ethics, in which every moral precept founded on reason is carried to a higher degree of purity and perfection, than in any other of the wisest philosophers of preceding ages; every moral pre-

cept

cept founded on falſe principles is totally
omitted, and many new precepts added peculiarly correſponding with the new object
of this religion.

Laſtly, That ſuch a ſyſtem of religion and
morality could not poſſibly have been the
work of any man, or ſet of men; much leſs
of thoſe obſcure, ignorant, and illiterate perſons, who actually did diſcover, and publiſh
it to the world; and that therefore it muſt
undoubtedly have been effected by the interpoſition of divine power, that is, that it
muſt derive its origin from God.

P R O-

PROPOSITION I.

VERY little need be faid to eftablifh my firft propofition, which is fingly this : That there is now extant a book intitled the New Teftament ; that is, there is a collection of writings diftinguifhed by that denomination, containing four hiftorical accounts of the birth, life, actions, difcourfes, and death of an extraordinary perfon named Jefus Chrift, who was born in the reign of Auguftus Cæfar, preached a new religion throughout the country of Judæa, and was put to a cruel and ignominious death in the reign of Tiberius. Alfo one other hiftorical account of the travels, tranfactions, and orations of fome mean and illiterate men, known by the title of his apoftles, whom he commiffioned to propagate his religion after his death ; which he foretold them he muft fuffer in confirmation of its truth. To thefe are added feveral epiftolary writings, addreffed addreſſed by theſe perſons to their fellow-labourers in this work, or to the ſeveral churches or ſocieties of Chriſtians, which they had eſtabliſhed in the ſeveral cities through which they had paſſed.

It would not be difficult to prove, that theſe books were written ſoon after thoſe extraordinary events, which are the ſubjects of them ; as we find them quoted, and referred to by an uninterrupted ſucceſſion of writers from thoſe to the preſent times : nor would it be leſs eaſy to ſhew, that the truth of all thoſe events, miracles only excepted, can no more be reaſonably queſtioned, than the truth of any other facts recorded in any hiſtory whatever : as there can be no more reaſon to doubt, that there exiſted ſuch a perſon as Jeſus Chriſt, ſpeaking, acting, and ſuffering in ſuch a manner as is there deſcribed, than that there were ſuch men as Tiberius, Herod, or Pontius Pilate, his cotemporaries ; or to ſuſpect, that Peter, Paul, and James were not the authors of thoſe epiſtles, to which their names are affixed,

than

than that Cicero and Pliny did not write those which are afcribed to them. It might alfo be made appear, that thefe books having been wrote by various perfons at different times, and in diftant places, could not poffibly have been the work of a fingle impoftor, nor of a fraudulent combination, being all ftamped with the fame marks of an uniform originality in their very frame and compofition.

But all thefe circumftances I fhall pafs over unobferved, as they do not fall in with the courfe of my argument, nor are neceffary for the fupport of it. Whether thefe books were wrote by the authors whofe names are prefixed to them, whether they have been enlarged, diminifhed, or any way corrupted by the artifice or ignorance of tranflators or tranfcribers; whether in the hiftorical parts the writers were inftructed by a perpetual, a partial, or by any infpiration at all; whether in the religious and moral parts, they received their doctrines from a divine influence, or from the inftructions

and

[handwritten margin note: Chapters not written by the titled name.]

and conversation of their master; whether in their facts or sentiments there is always the most exact agreement, or whether in both they sometimes differ from each other; whether they are in any case mistaken, or always infallible; or ever pretended to be so, I shall not here dispute : let the Deist avail himself of all these doubts and difficulties, and decide them in conformity to his own opinions, I shall not contend, because they affect not my argument: all that I assert is a plain fact, which cannot be denied, that such writings do now exist.

Point one
N.T. exists.

P R O-

PROPOSITION II.

MY second proposition is not quite so simple, but, I think, not less undeniable than the former, and is this: That from this book may be extracted a system of religion entirely new, both with regard to the object, and the doctrines, not only infinitely superior to, but totally unlike every thing, which had ever before entered into the mind of man: I say extracted, because all the doctrines of this religion having been delivered at various times, and on various occasions, and here only historically recorded, no uniform or regular system of theology is here to be found; and better perhaps it had been, if less labour had been employed by the learned, to bend and twist these divine materials into the polished forms of human systems, to which they never will submit, and for which they were never intended by their great author. Why he chose not to leave

5   any

any fuch behind him we know not, but it might poffibly be, becaufe he knew, that the imperfection of man was incapable of receiving fuch a fyftem, and that we are more properly, and more fafely conducted by the diftant and fcattered rays, than by the too powerful funfhine of divine illumination: " If I have told you earthly things," fays he, " and ye believe not, how fhall ye believe " if I tell you of heavenly things * ?" that is, If my inftructions concerning your behaviour in the prefent, as relative to a future life, are fo difficult to be underftood, that you can fcarcely believe me, how fhall you believe, if I endeavour to explain to you the nature of celeftial beings, the defigns of Providence, and the myfteries of his difpenfations; fubjects which you have neither ideas to comprehend, nor language to exprefs?

Firft then, the object of this religion is entirely new, and is this; to prepare us by a

object
new

* John iii. 12.

ftate

ftate of probation for the kingdom of heaven. This is every where profeffed by
Chrift and his apoftles to be the chief end
of the Chriftian's life ; the crown for which
he is to contend, the goal to which he is to
run, the harveft which is to pay him for all
his labours : Yet previous to their preaching
no fuch prize was ever hung out to mankind,
nor any means prefcribed for the attainment
of it.

It is indeed true, that fome of the philofophers of antiquity entertained notions of a
future ftate, but mixed with much doubt and
uncertainty : their legiflators alfo endeavoured to infufe into the minds of the people a
belief of rewards and punifhments after
death; but by this they only intended to
give a fanction to their laws, and to enforce
the practice of virtue for the benefit of mankind in the prefent life : this alone feems to
have been their end, and a meritorious end
it was; but Chriftianity not only operates
more effectually to this end, but has a nobler defign in view, which is, by a proper
education

education here to render us fit members of a celestial society hereafter. In all former religions the good of the present life was the first object; in the Christian it is but the second; in those, men were incited to promote that good by the hopes of a future reward; in this, the practice of virtue is injoined in order to qualify them for that reward. There is great difference, I apprehend, in these two plans, that is, in adhering to virtue from its present utility in expectation of future happiness, and living in such a manner as to qualify us for the acceptance and enjoyment of that happiness; and the conduct and dispositions of those, who act on these different principles, must be no less different: on the first, the constant practice of justice, temperance, and sobriety, will be sufficient; but on the latter, we must add to these an habitual piety, faith, resignation, and contempt of the world: the first may make us very good citizens, but will never produce a tolerable Christian. Hence it is that Christianity insists more strongly, than any

preceding

preceding inftitution religious or moral, on purity of heart and a benevolent difpofition ; becaufe thefe are abfolutely neceffary to its great end ; but in thofe whofe recommenda-tions of virtue regard the prefent life only, and whofe promifed rewards in another were low and fenfual, no preparatory qualifications were requifite to enable men to practife the one, or to enjoy the other : and therefore we fee this object is peculiar to this religion ; and with it was entirely new.

But although this object, and the princi-ple on which it is founded were new, and perhaps undifcoverable by reafon, yet when difcovered they are fo confonant to it, that we cannot but readily affent to them. For the truth of this principle, that the prefent life is a ftate of probation, and education to prepare us for another, is confirmed by every thing which we fee around us : it is the only key which can open to us the defigns of Providence in the œconomy of human af-fairs, the only clue, which can guide us through that pathlefs wildernefs, and the only plan on which this world could poſſibly have been formed, or on which the hiſtory of it can be comprehended or explained. It could never have been formed on a plan of happineſs: becauſe it is every where overſpread with innumerable miſeries; nor of miſery, becauſe it is interſperſed with many enjoyments: it could not have been conſtituted for a ſcene of wiſdom and virtue, becauſe the hiſtory of mankind is little more than a detail of their follies and wickedneſs: nor of vice, becauſe that is no plan at all, being deſtructive of all exiſtence, and conſequently of its own. But on this ſyſtem all that we here meet with, may be eaſily accounted for; for this mixture of happineſs and miſery, of virtue and vice, neceſſarily reſults from a ſtate of probation and education; as probation implies trials, ſufferings, and a capacity of offending, and education a propriety of chaſtiſement for thoſe offences.

In the next place, the doctrines of this religion are equally new with the object; and contain ideas of God, and of man, of the preſent,

fent, and of a future life ; and of the relations which all thefe bear to each other, totally unheard of, and quite diffimilar from
any which had ever been thought on, previous to its publication.   No other ever drew
fo juft a portrait of the worthleffnefs of this
world, and all its purfuits, nor exhibited fuch
diftinct, lively, and exquifite pictures of the
joys of another ; of the refurrection of the
dead, the laft judgment, and the triumphs
of the righteous in that tremendous day,
" when this corruptible fhall put on incor-
" ruption, and this mortal fhall put on im-
" mortality*."   No other has ever reprefented the Supreme Being in the character of three perfons united in one God †.

---

* 1 Cor. xv. 53.

† That there fubfifts fome fuch union in the divine
nature, the whole tenour of the New Teftament feems
to exprefs, and it was fo underftood in the earlieft
ages : but whether this union does, or does not imply
equality, or whether it fubfifts in general, or only in
particular circumftances, we are not informed, and
therefore on thefe queftions it is not only unneceffary,
but improper for us to decide.

No

No other has attempted to reconcile those seeming contradictory but both true propositions, the contingency of future events, and the foreknowledge of God, or the free will of the creature with the over-ruling grace of the Creator. No other has so fully declared the necessity of wickedness and punishment, yet so effectually instructed individuals to resist the one, and to escape the other : no other has ever pretended to give any account of the depravity of man, or to point out any remedy for it : no other has ventured to declare the unpardonable nature of sin without the influence of a mediatorial interposition, and a vicarious atonement from the sufferings of a superior being*.   Whether these wonderful doctrines

* That Christ suffered and died as an atonement for the sins of mankind, is a doctrine so constantly and so strongly enforced through every part of the New Testament, that whoever will seriously peruse those writings, and deny that it is there, may, with as much reason and truth, after reading the works of Thucydides and Livy, assert, that in them no mention is made of any facts relative to the histories of Greece and Rome.

are

are worthy of our belief muſt depend on the opinion, which we entertain of the authority of thoſe, who publiſhed them to the world; but certain it is, that they are all ſo far removed from every tract of the human imagination, that it ſeems equally impoſſible, that they ſhould ever have been derived from the knowledge or the artifice of man.

Some indeed there are, who, by perverting the eſtabliſhed ſignification of words, (which they call explaining) have ventured to expunge all theſe doctrines out of the ſcriptures, for no other reaſon than that they are not able to comprehend them; and argue thus:——The ſcriptures are the word of God; in his word no propoſitions contradictory to reaſon can have a place; theſe propoſitions are contradictory to reaſon, and therefore they are not there. But if theſe bold aſſertors would claim any regard, they ſhould reverſe their argument, and ſay,—— Theſe doctrines make a part, and a material part of the ſcriptures, they are contradictory to reaſon; no propoſitions contradictory to

reaſon

reason can be a part of the word of God, and therefore neither the scriptures, nor the pretended revelation contained in them, can be derived from him : This would be an argument worthy of rational and candid Deists, and demand a respectful attention ; but when men pretend to disprove facts by reasoning, they have no right to expect an answer.

And here I cannot omit observing, that the personal character of the author of this religion is no less new, and extraordinary, than the religion itself, who " spake as never " man spake *," and lived as never man lived : in proof of this, I do not mean to alledge, that he was born of a virgin, that he fasted forty days, that he performed a variety of miracles, and after being buried three days, that he arose from the dead ; because these accounts will have but little effect on the minds of unbelievers, who, if they believe not the religion, will give no credit to

* John vii. 46.

the

the relation of thefe facts; but I will prove
it from facts which cannot be difputed; for
inftance, he is the only founder of a religion
in the hiftory of mankind, which is totally
unconnected with all human policy and government, and therefore totally unconducive
to any worldly purpofe whatever : all others,
Mahomet, Numa, and even Mofes himfelf,
blended their religious inftitutions with their
civil, and by them obtained dominion over
their refpective people; but Chrift neither
aimed at, nor would accept of any fuch
power; he rejected every object, which all
other men purfue, and made choice of all
thofe which others fly from, and are afraid
of : he refufed power, riches, honours, and
pleafure, and courted poverty, ignominy,
tortures, and death. Many have been the
enthufiafts and impoftors, who have endeavoured to impofe on the world pretended revelations, and fome of them from pride, obftinacy, or principle, have gone fo far, as to
lay down their lives, rather than retract;
but I defy hiftory to fhew one, who ever

made

made his own sufferings and death a necessary part of his original plan, and essential to his mission; this Christ actually did, he foresaw, foretold, declared, their necessity, and voluntarily endured them. If we seriously contemplate the divine lessons, the perfect precepts, the beautiful discourses, and the consistent conduct of this wonderful person, we cannot possibly imagine, that he could have been either an idiot or a madman; and yet, if he was not what he pretended to be, he can be considered in no other light; and even under this character he would deserve some attention, because of so sublime and rational an insanity there is no other instance in the history of mankind.

If any one can doubt of the superior excellence of this religion above all which preceded it, let him but peruse with attention those unparalleled writings in which it is transmitted to the present times, and compare them with the most celebrated productions of the pagan world; and if he is not sensible of their superior beauty, simplicity,

and

and originality, I will venture to pronounce, that he is as deficient in taste as in faith, and that he is as bad a critic as a Christian : for in what school of ancient philosophy can he find a lesson of morality so perfect as Christ's sermon on the mount ? From which of them can he collect an address to the Deity so concise, and yet so comprehensive, so expressive of all that we want, and all that we could deprecate, as that short prayer, which he formed for, and recommended to his disciples ? From the works of what sage of antiquity can he produce so pathetic a recommendation of benevolence to the distressed, and enforced by such assurances of a reward, as in those words of Christ ? " Come, ye " blessed of my Father ! inherit the kingdom " prepared for you from the foundation of " the world : for I was an hungred, and ye " gave me meat ; I was thirsty, and ye gave " me drink ; I was a stranger, and ye took " me in ; I was naked, and ye clothed me ; " I was sick, and ye visited me ; I was in " prison, and ye came unto me. Then shall

" the

" the righteous anfwer him, faying—Lord,
" when faw we thee an hungred, and fed
" thee, or thirfty, and gave thee drink ? when
" faw we thee a ftranger, and took thee in,
" or naked, and clothed thee ? or when faw
" we thee fick and in prifon, and came unto
" thee ? Then fhall I anfwer and fay unto
" them,—Verily I fay unto you, inafmuch
" as you have done it to the leaft of thefe
" my brethren, ye have done it unto me *."
Where is there fo juft, and fo elegant a reproof
of eagernefs and anxiety in worldly purfuits,
clofed with fo forcible an exhortation to confidence in the goodnefs of our Creator, as in
thefe words ?—" Behold the fowls of the air ;
" for they fow not, neither do they reap, nor
" gather into barns, yet your heavenly Fa-
" ther feedeth them. Are ye not much bet-
" ter than they ? Confider the lilies of the
" field, how they grow; they toil not, nei-
" ther do they fpin ; and yet I fay unto you,
" that even Solomon in all his glory was not

* Matt. xxv. 34.

" arrayed

examples.

" arrayed like one of these : wherefore, if
" God so clothe the grass of the field, which
" to-day is, and to-morrow is cast into the
" oven, shall he not much more clothe you?
" O ye of little faith *!" By which of their
most celebrated poets are the joys reserved
for the righteous in a future state, so sub-
limely described, as by this short declaration,
that they are superior to all description?
" Eye hath not seen, nor ear heard, neither
" have entered into the heart of man, the
" things, which God hath prepared for them
" that love him †." Where amidst the dark
clouds of pagan philosophy can he shew us
such a clear prospect of a future state, the
immortality of the soul, the resurrection of
the dead, and the general judgment, as in
St. Paul's first epistle to the Corinthians?
Or from whence can he produce such co-
gent exhortations to the practice of every
virtue, such ardent incitements to piety and
devotion, and such assistances to attain them,

---

* Matt. vi. 26, 28. † 1 Cor. ii. 9.]

as thofe which are to be met with throughout every page of thefe inimitable writings? To quote all the paffages in them relative to thefe fubjects, would be almoft to tranfcribe the whole; it is fufficient to obferve, that they are every where ftamped with fuch apparent marks of fupernatural affiftance, as render them indifputably fuperior to, and totally unlike all human compofitions whatever; and this fuperiority and diffimilarity is ftill more ftrongly marked by one remarkable circumftance peculiar to themfelves, which is, that whilft the moral parts, being of the moft general ufe, are intelligible to the meaneft capacities, the learned and inquifitive throughout all ages, perpetually find in them inexhauftible difcoveries, concerning the nature, attributes, and difpenfations of Providence.

To fay the truth, before the appearance of Chriftianity there exifted nothing like religion on the face of the earth; the Jewifh only excepted: all other nations were immerfed in the groffeft idolatry, which had
little

little or no connection with morality, except to corrupt it by the infamous examples of their imaginary deities: they all worshipped a multiplicity of gods and dæmons, whose favour they courted by impious, obscene, and ridiculous ceremonies, and whose anger they endeavoured to appease by the most abominable cruelties. In the politest ages of the politest nations in the world, at a time when Greece and Rome had carried the arts of oratory, poetry, history, architecture, and sculpture to the highest perfection, and made no inconsiderable advances in those of mathematics, natural, and even moral philosophy, in religious knowledge they had made none at all; a strong presumption, that the noblest efforts of the mind of man, unassisted by revelation, were unequal to the task. Some few indeed of their philosophers were wise enough to reject these general absurdities, and dared to attempt a loftier flight: Plato introduced many sublime ideas of nature, and its first cause, and of the immortality of the soul, which being above his own and all

human

human difcovery, he probably acquired from the books of Mofes or the converfation of fome Jewifh rabbies, which he might have met with in Egypt, where he refided, and ftudied for feveral years: from him Ariftotle, and from both Cicero and fome few others drew moft amazing ftores of philofophical fcience, and carried their refearches into divine truths as far as human genius alone could penetrate. But thefe were bright conftellations, which appeared fingly in feveral centuries, and even thefe with all this knowledge were very deficient in true theology. From the vifible works of the creation they traced the being and principal attributes of the Creator; but the relation which his being and attributes bear to man they little underftood; of piety and devotion they had fcarce any fenfe, nor could they form any mode of worfhip worthy of the purity and perfection of the divine nature: they occafionally flung out many elegant encomiums on the native beauty, and excellence of virtue: but they founded it not

5

on

on the commands of God, nor connected it with a holy life, nor hung out the happiness of heaven as its reward, or its object. They sometimes talked of virtue carrying men to heaven, and placing them amongst the gods ; but by this virtue they meant only the invention of arts, or feats of arms : for with them heaven was open only to legislators, and conquerors, the civilizers, or destroyers of mankind. This was then the summit of religion in the most polished nations in the world, and even this was confined to a few philosophers, prodigies of genius and literature, who were little attended to, and less understood by the generality of mankind in their own countries ; whilst all the rest were involved in one common cloud of ignorance and superstition.

At this time Christianity broke forth from the east like a rising sun, and dispelled this universal darkness, which obscured every part of the globe, and even at this day prevails in all those remoter regions, to which

its

its falutary influence has not as yet extended. From all thofe which it has reached, it has notwithftanding its corruptions, banifhed all thofe enormities, and introduced a more rational devotion, and purer morals : it has taught men the unity, and attributes of the Supreme Being, the remiffion of fins, the refurrection of the dead, life everlafting, and the kingdom of heaven ; doctrines as inconceivable to the wifeft of mankind, antecedent to its appearance, as the Newtonian fyftem is at this day to the moft ignorant tribes of favages in the wilds of America ; doctrines, which human reafon never could have difcovered, but which when difcovered, coincide with, and are confirmed by it ; and which, though beyond the reach of all the learning and penetration of Plato, Ariftotle, and Cicero, are now clearly laid open to the eye of every peafant and mechanic with the bible in his hand. Thefe are all plain facts too glaring to be contradicted, and therefore, whatever we may think of the authority of thefe

these books, the relations which they contain, or the infpiration of their authors, of
thefe facts no man, who has eyes to read,
or ears to hear, can entertain a doubt; becaufe there are the books, and in them is this
religion.

PROPOSITION III.

MY third proposition is this ; That from this book called the New Testament, may be collected a system of ethics, in which every moral precept founded on reason is carried to a higher degree of purity and perfection, than in any other of the antient philosophers of preceding ages ; every moral precept founded on false principles is entirely omitted, and many new precepts added, peculiarly corresponding with the new object of this religion.

By moral precepts founded on reason, I mean all those, which enforce the practice of such duties as reason informs us must improve our natures, and conduce to the happiness of mankind : such are piety to God, benevolence to men, justice, charity, temperance, and sobriety, with all those, which prohibit the commission of the contrary vices, all which debase our natures, and, by mutual

injuries,

injuries, introduce univerſal diſorder, and conſequently univerſal miſery. By precepts founded on falſe principles, I mean thoſe which recommend fictitious virtues productive of none of theſe ſalutary effects, and therefore, however celebrated and admired, are in fact no virtues at all; ſuch are valour, patriotiſm, and friendſhip.

That virtues of the firſt kind are carried to a higher degree of purity and perfection by the Chriſtian religion than by any other, it is here unneceſſary to prove, becauſe this is a truth, which has been frequently demonſtrated by her friends, and never once denied by the moſt determined of her adverſaries; but it will be proper to ſhew, that thoſe of the latter ſort are moſt judiciouſly omitted; becauſe they have really no intrinſic merit in them, and are totally incompatible with the genius and ſpirit of this inſtitution.

Valour, for inſtance, or active courage, is for the moſt part conſtitutional, and therefore can have no more claim to moral merit, than wit, beauty, health, ſtrength, or any

other

other endowment of the mind or body; and so far is it from producing any salutary effects by introducing peace, order, or happiness into society, that it is the usual perpetrator of all the violences, which from retaliated injuries distract the world with bloodshed and devastation. It is the engine by which the strong are enabled to plunder the weak, the proud to trample upon the humble, and the guilty to oppress the innocent; it is the chief instrument which Ambition employs in her unjust pursuits of wealth and power, and is therefore so much extolled by her votaries: it was indeed congenial with the religion of pagans, whose gods were for the most part made out of deceased heroes, exalted to heaven as a reward for the mischiefs which they had perpetrated upon earth, and therefore with them this was the first of virtues, and had even engrossed that denomination to itself; but whatever merit it may have assumed among pagans, with Christians it can pretend to none, and few or none are the occasions in which they are

permitted

permitted to exert it : they are fo far from being allowed to inflict evil, that they are forbid even to refift it : they are fo far from being encouraged to revenge injuries, that one of their firft duties is to forgive them ; fo far from being incited to deftroy their enemies, that they are commanded to love them, and to ferve them to the utmoft of their power. If Chriftian nations therefore were nations of Chriftians, all war would be impoffible and unknown amongft them, and valour could be neither of ufe nor eftimation, and therefore could never have a place in the catalogue of Chriftian virtues, being irreconcileable with all its precepts. I object not to the praife and honours beftowed on the valiant, they are the leaft tribute which can be paid them by thofe who enjoy fafety and affluence by the intervention of their dangers and fufferings : I affert only that active courage can never be a Chriftian virtue, becaufe a Chriftian can have nothing to do with it. Paffive courage is indeed frequently, and properly inculcated by this

meek

meek and suffering religion, under the titles
of patience and resignation : a real and sub-
stantial virtue this, and a direct contrast to
the former ; for passive courage arises from
the noblest dispositions of the human mind,
from a contempt of misfortunes, pain, and
death, and a confidence in the protection of
the Almighty ; active, from the meanest ;
from passion, vanity, and self-dependence :
passive courage is derived from a zeal for
truth, and a perseverance in duty ; active, is
the offspring of pride and revenge, and the
parent of cruelty and injustice : in short,
passive courage is the resolution of a philosopher ; active, the ferocity of a savage. Nor
is this more incompatible with the precepts,
than with the object of this religion, which
is the attainment of the kingdom of heaven ;
for valour is not that sort of violence, by
which that kingdom is to be taken ; nor are
the turbulent spirits of heroes and conquerors admissible into those regions of
peace, subordination, and tranquillity.

Patriotism also, that celebrated virtue so
much

much practised in antient, and so much professed in modern times, that virtue, which so
long preserved the liberties of Greece, and
exalted Rome to the empire of the world:
this celebrated virtue, I say, must also be
excluded; because it not only falls short
of, but directly counteracts, the extensive
benevolence of this religion. A Christian
is of no country, he is a citizen of the world,
and his neighbours and countrymen are the
inhabitants of the remotest regions, whenever their distresses demand his friendly assistance: Christianity commands us to love
all mankind, patriotism to oppress all other
countries to advance the imaginary prosperity of our own: Christianity enjoins us to
imitate the universal benevolence of our
Creator, who pours forth his blessings on
every nation upon earth; patriotism, to copy
the mean partiality of an English parish of-
ficer, who thinks injustice and cruelty meritorious, whenever they promote the interests
of his own inconsiderable village. This
has ever been a favourite virtue with man-

kind,

kind, becauſe it conceals ſelf-intereſt under the maſk of public ſpirit, not only from others, but even from themſelves, and gives a licence to inflict wrongs and injuries not only with impunity, but with applauſe; but it is ſo diametrically oppoſite to the great characteriſtic of this inſtitution, that it never could have been admitted into the liſt of Chriſtian virtues.

Friendſhip likewiſe, although more congenial to the principles of Chriſtianity, ariſing from more tender and amiable diſpoſitions, could never gain admittance amongſt her benevolent precepts, for the ſame reaſon; becauſe it is too narrow and confined, and appropriates that benevolence to a ſingle object, which is here commanded to be extended over all. Where friendſhips ariſe from ſimilarity of ſentiments, and diſintereſted affections, they are advantageous, agreeable, and innocent, but have little pretenſions to merit; for it is juſtly obſerved, " If ye love them, which love you, what " thanks have ye? for ſinners alſo love thoſe,

" that

" that love them *." But if they are formed from alliances in parties, factions, and interests, or from a participation of vices, the usual parents of what are called friendships among mankind, they are then both mischievous and criminal, and consequently forbidden; but in their utmost purity deserve no recommendation from this religion.

To the judicious omission of these false virtues we may add that remarkable silence, which the Christian legislator every where preserves on subjects esteemed by all others of the highest importance, civil government, national policy, and the rights of war and peace; of these he has not taken the least notice, probably for this plain reason, because it would have been impossible to have formed any explicit regulations concerning them, which must not have been inconsistent with the purity of his religion, or with the practical observance of such imperfect crea-

* Luke vi. 32.

tures

tures as men ruling over, and contending
with each other: for inftance, had he abfolutely forbid all refiftance to the reigning
powers, he had conftituted a plan of defpo-
tifm, and made men flaves; had he allowed
it, he muft have authorifed difobedience,
and made them rebels : had he in direct
terms prohibited all war, he muft have left
his followers for ever an eafy prey to every
infidel invader; had he permitted it, he
muft have licenfed all that rapine and murder, with which it is unavoidably attended.

Let us now examine what are thofe new
precepts in this religion peculiarly correfponding with the new object of it, that is,
preparing us for the kingdom of heaven: of
thefe the chief are poornefs of fpirit, for-
givenefs of injuries, and charity to all men;
to thefe we may add repentance, faith, felf-
abafement, and a detachment from the
world, all moral duties peculiar to this religion, and abfolutely neceffary to the attainment of its end.

"Bleffed

" Blessed are the poor in spirit ; for theirs
" is the kingdom of heaven *:" by which
poorness of spirit is to be understood a disposition of mind, meek, humble, submissive
to power, void of ambition, patient of injuries, and free from all resentment. This was
so new, and so opposite to the ideas of all
pagan moralists, that they thought this temper of mind a criminal and contemptible
meanness, which must induce men to sacri-
fice the glory of their country, and their own
honour, to a shameful pusillanimity ; and such
it appears to almost all who are called Christians even at this day, who not only reject it
in practice, but disavow it in principle, notwithstanding this explicit declaration of their
master. We see them revenging the smallest
affronts by premeditated murder, as individuals, on principles of honour ; and, in their
national capacities, destroying each other
with fire and sword, for the low considerations of commercial interests, the balance of

* Matt. v. 3.

rival

rival powers, or the ambition of princes: we see them with their laſt breath animating each other to a ſavage revenge, and, in the agonies of death, plunging with feeble arms their daggers into the hearts of their opponents: and, what is ſtill worſe, we hear all theſe barbariſms celebrated by hiſtorians, flattered by poets, applauded in theatres, approved in ſenates, and even ſanctified in pulpits. But univerſal practice cannot alter the nature of things, nor univerſal error change the nature of truth: pride was not made for man; but humility, meekneſs, and reſignation, that is poorneſs of ſpirit, was made for man; and properly belongs to his dependent and precarious ſituation; and is the only diſpoſition of mind, which can enable him to enjoy eaſe and quiet here, and happineſs hereafter: yet was this important precept entirely unknown until it was promulgated by him, who ſaid, " Suffer little children to " come unto me, and forbid them not; for " of ſuch is the kingdom of heaven: Verily " I ſay unto you, whoever ſhall not receive
" the

" the kingdom of God as a little child, he
" shall not enter therein *."

Another precept, equally new and no less
excellent, is forgiveness of injuries: " Ye
" have heard," says Christ to his disciples,
" Thou shalt love thy neighbour, and hate
" thine enemy; but I say unto you, love
" your enemies; bless them that curse you, do
" good to them that hate you, and pray for
" them which despitefully use you, and per-
" secute you †." This was a lesson so new,
and so utterly unknown, till taught by his
doctrines, and enforced by his example, that
the wisest moralists of the wisest nations and
ages represented the desire of revenge as a
mark of a noble mind, and the accomplish-
ment of it as one of the chief felicities attendant on a fortunate man. But how much
more magnanimous, how much more beneficial to mankind, is forgiveness! it is more
magnanimous, because every generous and
exalted disposition of the human mind is re-

* Matt. x. 14.   † Matt. v. 43.

quisite

quifite to the practice of it: for thefe alone can enable us to bear the wrongs and infults of wickednefs and folly with patience, and to look down on the perpetrators of them with pity, rather than indignation; thefe alone can teach us, that fuch are but a part of thofe fufferings allotted to us in this ftate of probation, and to know, that to overcome evil with good, is the moft glorious of all victories: it is the moft beneficial, becaufe this amiable conduct alone can put an end to an eternal fucceffion of injuries and retaliations; for every retaliation becomes a new injury, and requires another act of revenge for fatisfaction. But would we obferve this falutary precept, to love our enemies, and to do good to thofe who defpitefully ufe us, this obftinate benevolence would at laft conquer the moft inveterate hearts, and we fhould have no enemies to forgive. How much more exalted a character therefore is a Chriftian martyr, fuffering with refignation, and praying for the guilty, than that of a Pagan hero, breathing revenge, and deftroying the innocent!

innocent! Yet, noble and useful as this virtue is, before the appearance of this religion it was not only unpractised, but decried in principle as mean and ignominious, though so obvious a remedy for most of the miseries of this life, and so necessary a qualification for the happiness of another.

A third precept, first noticed and first enjoined by this institution, is charity to all men. What this is, we may best learn from this admirable description, painted in the following words : " Charity suffereth long " and is kind ; charity envieth not ; charity " vaunteth not itself ; is not puffed up ; doth " not behave itself unseemly ; seeketh not " her own ; is not easily provoked ; think-" eth no evil ; rejoiceth not in iniquity, but " rejoiceth in truth ; feareth all things ; be-" lieveth all things ; hopeth all things ; en-" dureth all things*." Here we have an accurate delineation of this bright constellation of all virtues ; which consists not, as

* 1 Cor. xiii. 4.

many

many imagine, in the building of monafteries, endowment of hofpitals, or the diftribution of alms; but in fuch an amiable difpofition of mind, as exercifes itfelf every hour in acts of kindnefs, patience, complacency, and benevolence to all around us, and which alone is able to promote happinefs in the prefent life, or render us capable of receiving it in another: and yet this is totally new, and fo it is declared to be by the author of it: " A new commandment I " give unto you, that ye love one another; " as I have loved you, that ye love one ano- " ther; by this fhall all men know that ye " are my difciples, if ye have love one to " another *." This benevolent difpofition is made the great characteriftic of a Chriftian, the teft of his obedience, and the mark by which he is to be diftinguifhed. This love for each other is that charity juft now defcribed, and contains all thofe qualities, which are there attributed to it; humility,

* John xiii. 34.

patience,

patience, meekneſs, and beneficence : without which we muſt live in perpetual diſcord,
and conſequently cannot pay obedience to
this commandment by loving one another ;
a commandment ſo ſublime, ſo rational, and
ſo beneficial, ſo wiſely calculated to correct
the depravity, diminiſh the wickedneſs, and
abate the miſeries of human nature, that, did
we univerſally comply with it, we ſhould
ſoon be relieved from all the inquietudes
ariſing from our own unruly paſſions, anger,
envy, revenge, malice, and ambition, as well
as from all thoſe injuries to which we are
perpetually expoſed from the indulgence of
the ſame paſſions in others. It would alſo
preſerve our minds in ſuch a ſtate of tranquillity, and ſo prepare them for the kingdom of héaven, that we ſhould ſlide out of a
life of peace, love, and benevolence, into
that celeſtial ſociety, by an almoſt imper-
ceptible tranſition. Yet was this commandment entirely new, when given by him, who ſo
intitles it, and has made it the capital duty
of his religion, becauſe the moſt indiſpenſa-

bly neceſſary to the attainment of its great object, the kingdom of heaven; into which if proud, turbulent, and vindictive ſpirits were permitted to enter, they muſt unavoidably deſtroy the happineſs of that ſtate by the operations of the ſame paſſions and vices, by which they diſturb the preſent; and therefore all ſuch muſt be eternally excluded, not only as a puniſhment, but alſo from incapacity.

Repentance, by this we plainly ſee, is another new moral duty ſtrenuouſly inſiſted on by this religion, and by no other, becauſe abſolutely neceſſary to the accompliſhment of its end; for this alone can purge us from thoſe tranſgreſſions, from which we cannot be totally exempted in this ſtate of trial and temptation, and purify us from that depravity in our nature, which renders us incapable of attaining this end. Hence alſo we may learn, that no repentance can remove this incapacity, but ſuch as entirely changes the nature and diſpoſition of the offender; which in the language of ſcripture is called " being born again." Mere contrition for

5

paſt crimes, nor even the pardon of them, cannot effect this, unleſs it operates to this entire converſion or new birth, as it is properly and emphatically named : for ſorrow can no more purify a mind corrupted by a long continuance in vicious habits, than it can reſtore health to a body diſtempered by a long courſe of vice and intemperance. Hence alſo every one, who is in the leaſt acquainted with himſelf, may judge of the reaſonableneſs of the hope that is in him, and of his ſituation in a future ſtate by that of his preſent.   If he feels in himſelf a temper proud, turbulent, vindictive, and malevolent, and a violent attachment to the pleaſures or buſineſs of the world, he may be aſſured, that he muſt be excluded from the kingdom of heaven ; not only becauſe his conduct can merit no ſuch reward, but becauſe, if admitted, he would find there no objects ſatisfactory to his paſſions, inclinations, and purſuits, and therefore could only diſturb the happineſs of others without enjoying any ſhare of it himſelf.

Faith

Faith is another moral duty injoined by this inſtitution, of a ſpecies ſo new, that the philoſophers of antiquity had no word expreſſive of this idea, nor any ſuch idea to be expreſſed; for the word πιστις or *fides*, which we tranſlate faith, was never uſed by any pagan writer in a ſenſe the leaſt ſimilar to that, to which it is applied in the New Teſtament: where in general it ſignifies an humble, teachable, and candid diſpoſition, a truſt in God, and confidence in his promiſes; when applied particularly to Chriſtianity, it means no more than a belief of this ſingle propoſition, That Chriſt was the ſon of God; that is, in the language of thoſe writings, the Meſſiah, who was foretold by the prophets, and expected by the Jews; who was ſent by God into the world to preach righteouſneſs, judgment, and everlaſting life, and to die as an atonement for the ſins of mankind. This was all that Chriſt required to be believed by thoſe who were willing to become his diſciples: he, who does not believe this, is not a Chriſtian, and he who does, believes the whole

whole that is effential to his profeffion, and all that is properly comprehended under the name of faith. This unfortunate word has indeed been fo tortured and fo mifapplied to mean every abfurdity, which artifice could impofe upon ignorance, that it has loft all pretenfions to the title of virtue ; but if brought back to the fimplicity of its original fignification, it well deferves that name, becaufe it ufually arifes from the moft amiable difpofitions, and is always a direct contraft to pride, obftinacy, and felf-conceit. If taken in the extenfive fenfe of an affent to the evidence of things not feen, it comprehends the exiftence of a God, and a future ftate, and is therefore not only itfelf a moral virtue, but the fource from whence all others muft proceed ; for on the belief of thefe all religion and morality muft entirely depend. It cannot be altogether void of moral merit, (as fome would reprefent it) becaufe it is in a degree voluntary ; for daily experience fhews us, that men not only pretend to, but actually do believe, and difbe-

E 3   lieve,

lieve, almoſt any propoſitions, which beſt ſuit their intereſts, or inclinations, and unfeign-edly change their ſincere opinions with their ſituations and circumſtances. For we have power over the mind's eye, as well as over the body's, to ſhut it againſt the ſtrongeſt rays of truth and religion, whenever they be-come painful to us, and to open it again to the faint glimmerings of ſcepticiſm and infi-delity when we " love darkneſs rather than " light, becauſe our deeds are evil *." And this, I think, ſufficiently refutes all objections to the moral nature of faith, drawn from the ſuppoſition of its being quite involuntary, and neceſſarily dependent on the degree of evidence, which is offered to our underſtand-ings.

Self-abaſement is another moral duty in-culcated by this religion only ; which re-quires us to impute even our own virtues to the grace and favour of our Creator, and to acknowledge, that we can do nothing good by our own powers, unleſs aſſiſted by his

* John iii. 19.

over-

over-ruling influence. This doctrine seems at first sight to infringe on our free-will, and to deprive us of all merit; but, on a closer examination, the truth of it may be demonstrated both by reason and experience, and that in fact it does not impair the one, or depreciate the other: and that it is productive of so much humility, resignation, and dependance on God, that it justly claims a place amongst the most illustrious moral virtues. Yet was this duty utterly repugnant to the proud and self-sufficient principles of the antient philosophers as well as modern Deists, and therefore before the publication of the gospel totally unknown and uncomprehended.

Detachment from the world is another moral virtue constituted by this religion alone: so new, that even at this day few of its professors can be persuaded, that it is required, or that it is any virtue at all. By this detachment from the world is not to be understood a seclusion from society, abstraction from all business, or retirement to a

gloomy

gloomy cloyfter. Induftry and labour, chear-
fulnefs and hofpitality are frequently recommended : nor is the acquifition of wealth and
honours prohibited, if they can be obtained
by honeft means, and a moderate degree of
attention and care : but fuch an unremitted
anxiety, and perpetual application as en-
groffes our whole time and thoughts, are
forbid, becaufe they are incompatible with
the fpirit of this religion, and muft utterly
difqualify us for the attainment of its great
end. We toil on in the vain purfuits and
frivolous occupations of the world, die in
our harnefs, and then expect, if no gigantic
crime ftands in the way, to ftep immediately
into the kingdom of heaven : but this is impoffible ; for without a previous detachment
from the bufinefs of this world, we cannot
be prepared for the happinefs of another.
Yet this could make no part of the morality
of pagans, becaufe their virtues were altogether connected with this bufinefs, and con-
fifted chiefly in conducting it with honour to
themfelves, and benefit to the public : but
Chriftianity

Chriſtianity has a nobler object in view, which, if not attended to, muſt be loſt for ever. This object is that celeſtial manſion of which we ſhould never loſe ſight, and to which we ſhould be ever advancing during our journey through life : but this by no means precludes us from performing the buſineſs, or enjoying the amuſements of travellers, provided they detain us not too long, or lead us too far out of our way.

It cannot be denied, that the great author of the Chriſtian inſtitution, firſt and ſingly ventured to oppoſe all the chief principles of pagan virtue, and to introduce a religion directly oppoſite to thoſe erroneous though long-eſtabliſhed opinions, both in its duties and in its object. The moſt celebrated virtues of the ancients were high ſpirit, intrepid courage, and implacable reſentment.

Impiger, iracundus, inexorabilis, acer,

was the portrait of the moſt illuſtrious hero, drawn by one of the firſt poets of antiquity. To all theſe admired qualities, thoſe of a true Chriſtian are an exact contraſt ; for this

religion

religion conſtantly enjoins poorneſs of ſpirit, meekneſs, patience, and forgiveneſs of injuries. "But I ſay unto you, that ye reſiſt "not evil; but whoever ſhall ſmite thee on "the right cheek, turn to him the other "alſo *." The favourite characters among the Pagans were the turbulent, ambitious, and intrepid, who through toils and dangers acquired wealth, and ſpent it in luxury, magnificence, and corruption; but both theſe are equally adverſe to the Chriſtian ſyſtem, which forbids all extraordinary efforts to obtain wealth, care to ſecure, or thought concerning the enjoyment of it. "Lay not "up for yourſelves treaſures on earth, &c." "Take no thought, ſaying, what ſhall we "eat, or what ſhall we drink, or wherewithal "ſhall we be cloathed? for after all theſe "things do the Gentiles ſeek †." The chief object of the Pagans was immortal fame: for this their poets ſang, their heroes fought, and their patriots died; and this was hung out by their philoſophers and legiſla-

* Matt. v. 39.   † Matt. vi. 31.

tors,

tors, as the great incitement to all noble and virtuous deeds. But what fays the Chriftian legiflator to his difciples on this fubject?
" Bleffed are ye, when men fhall revile you,
" and fhall fay all manner of evil againft you
" for my fake; rejoice, and be exceeding glad,
" for great is your reward in heaven *." So widely different is the genius of the Pagan and Chriftian morality, that I will venture to affirm, that the moft celebrated virtues of the former are more oppofite to the fpirit, and more inconfiftent with the end of the latter, than even their moft infamous vices; and that a Brutus wrenching vengeance out of his hands to whom alone it belongs, by murdering the oppreffor of his country, or a Cato murdering himfelf from an impatience of controul, leaves the world more unqualified for, and more inadmiffible into the kingdom of heaven, than even a Meffalina, or an Heliogabalus, with all their profligacy about them.

Nothing, I believe, has fo much contri-

* Matt. v. 11.

buted

buted to corrupt the true spirit of the Christian institution, as that partiality, which we contract from our earliest education for the manners of pagan antiquity: from whence we learn to adopt every moral idea, which is repugnant to it; to applaud false virtues, which that disavows; to be guided by laws of honour, which that abhors; to imitate characters, which that detests; and to behold heroes, patriots, conquerors, and suicides with admiration, whose conduct that utterly condemns. From a coalition of these opposite principles was generated that monstrous system of cruelty and benevolence, of barbarism and civility, of rapine and justice, of fighting and devotion, of revenge and generosity, which harrassed the world for several centuries with crusades, holy wars, knight-errantry, and single combats, and even still retains influence enough, under the name of honour, to defeat the most beneficent ends of this holy institution. I mean not by this to pass any censure on the principles of valour, patriotism, or honour:

they

they may be useful, and perhaps necessary, in the commerce and business of the present turbulent and imperfect state; and those who are actuated by them may be virtuous, honest, and even religious men: all that I assert is, that they cannot be Christians. A profligate may be a Christian, though a bad one, because he may be overpowered by passions and temptations, and his actions may contradict his principles; but a man, whose ruling principle is honour, however virtuous he may be, cannot be a Christian, because he erects a standard of duty, and deliberately adheres to it, diametrically opposite to the whole tenour of that religion.

The contrast between the Christian, and all other institutions religious or moral, previous to its appearance, is sufficiently evident, and surely the superiority of the former is as little to be disputed; unless any one shall undertake to prove, that humility, patience, forgiveness, and benevolence are less amiable, and less beneficial qualities, than pride, turbulence, revenge, and malignity:

nity: that the contempt of riches is lefs noble, than the acquifition by fraud and vil-
lainy, or the diftribution of them to the poor,
lefs commendable than avarice or profufion;
or that a real immortality in the kingdom of
heaven is an object lefs exalted, lefs rational,
and lefs worthy of purfuit, than an imaginary immortality in the applaufe of men:
that worthlefs tribute, which the folly of one
part of mankind pays to the wickednefs of
the other; a tribute, which a wife man ought
always to defpife, becaufe a good man can
fcarce ever obtain.

CON-

CONCLUSION.

IF I miſtake not, I have now fully eſtabliſhed the truth of my three propoſitions.

Firſt, That there is now extant a book intitled the New Teſtament.

Secondly, That from this book may be extracted a ſyſtem of religion entirely new; both in its object, and its doctrines, not only ſuperior to, but totally unlike every thing, which had ever before entered into the mind of man.

Thirdly, That from this book may likewiſe be collected a ſyſtem of ethics, in which every moral precept founded on reaſon is carried to a higher degree of purity and perfection, than in any other of the wiſeſt philoſophers of preceding ages; every moral precept founded on falſe principles totally omitted, and many new precepts added, peculiarly

culiarly correfponding with the new object of
this religion.

Every one of thefe propofitions, I am perfuaded, is incontrovertibly true; and if true,
this fhort, but certain conclufion muft inevitably follow; That fuch a fyftem of religion and morality could not poffibly have
been the work of any man, or fet of men,
much lefs of thofe obfcure, ignorant, and illiterate perfons who actually did difcover,
and publifh it to the world; and that therefore it muft have been effected by the fupernatural interpofition of divine power and
wifdom; that is, that it muft derive its origin
from God.

This argument feems to me little fhort of
demonftration, and is indeed founded on the
very fame reafoning, by which the material
world is proved to be the work of his invifi-
ble hand. We view with admiration the
heavens and the earth, and all therein contained; we contemplate with amazement the
minute bodies of animals too fmall for per-
ception

ception, and the immenſe planetary orbs too
vaſt for imagination: We are certain that
theſe cannot be the works of man; and
therefore we conclude with reaſon, that they
muſt be the productions of an omnipotent
Creator. In the ſame manner we ſee here a
ſcheme of religion and morality unlike and
ſuperior to all ideas of the human mind,
equally impoſſible to have been diſcovered
by the knowledge, as invented by the artifice
of man; and therefore by the very ſame
mode of reaſoning, and with the ſame juſtice,
we conclude, that it muſt derive its origin
from the ſame omnipotent and omniſcient
Being.

Nor was the propagation of this religion
leſs extraordinary than the religion itſelf, or
leſs above the reach of all human power, than
the diſcovery of it was above that of all human underſtanding. It is well known, that
in the courſe of a very few years it was
ſpread over all the principal parts of Aſia
and of Europe, and this by the miniſtry
only of an inconſiderable number of the

moſt inconſiderable perſons; that at this
time Paganiſm was in the higheſt repute,
believed univerſally by the vulgar, and pa-
troniſed by the great; that the wiſeſt men
of the wiſeſt nations aſſiſted at its ſacrifices, and conſulted its oracles on the moſt
important occaſions: Whether theſe were
the tricks of the prieſts or of the devil, is of
no conſequence, as they were both equally
unlikely to be converted, or overcome; the
fact is certain, that on the preaching of a
few fiſhermen, their altars were deſerted, and
their deities were dumb. This miracle they
undoubtedly performed, whatever we may
think of the reſt: and this is ſurely ſufficient
to prove the authority of their commiſſion;
and to convince us, that neither their undertaking nor the execution of it could poſſibly
be their own.

How much this divine inſtitution has
been corrupted, or how ſoon theſe corruptions began, how far it has been diſcoloured
by the falſe notions of illiterate ages, or
blended with fictions by pious frauds, or
how

how early thefe notions and fictions were introduced, no learning or fagacity is now able
precifely to afcertain ; but furely no man,
who ferioufly confiders the excellence and
novelty of its doctrines, the manner in which
it was at firft propagated through the world,
the perfons who atchieved that wonderful
work, and the originality of thofe writings
in which it is ftill recorded, can poffibly believe that it could ever have been the production of impofture, or chance ; or that
from an impofture the moft wicked and
blafphemous (for if an impofture, fuch it is)
all the religion and virtue now exifting on
earth can derive their fource.

But notwithftanding what has been here
urged, if any man can believe, that at a time
when the literature of Greece and Rome,
then in their meridian luftre, were infuffi-
cient for the tafk, the fon of a carpenter, together with twelve of the meaneft and moft
illiterate mechanics, his affociates, unaffifted
by any fupernatural power, fhould be able
to difcover or invent a fyftem of theology

F 2   the

the moſt ſublime, and of ethics the moſt perfect, which had eſcaped the penetration and
learning of Plato, Ariſtotle, and Cicero; and
that from this ſyſtem, by their own ſagacity,
they had excluded every falſe virtue, though
univerſally admired, and admitted every true
virtue, though deſpiſed and ridiculed by all
the reſt of the world : If any one can believe
that theſe men could become impoſtors, for
no other purpoſe than the propagation of
truth, villains for no end but to teach ho-
neſty, and martyrs without the leaſt proſpect
of honour or advantage; or that, if all this
ſhould have been poſſible, theſe few inconſiderable perſons ſhould have been able, in
the courſe of a few years, to have ſpread this
their religion over moſt parts of the then
known world, in oppoſition to the intereſts,
pleaſures, ambition, prejudices, and even
reaſon of mankind; to have triumphed over
the power of princes, the intrigues of ſtates,
the force of cuſtom, the blindneſs of zeal,
the influence of prieſts, the arguments of
orators, and the philoſophy of the world,
without

without any supernatural assistance; if any one can believe all these miraculous events, contradictory to the constant experience of the powers and dispositions of human nature, he must be possessed of much more faith than is necessary to make him a Christian, and remain an unbeliever from mere credulity.

But should these credulous infidels after all be in the right, and this pretended revelation be all a fable; from believing it what harm could ensue? Would it render princes more tyrannical, or subjects more ungovernable? the rich more insolent, or the poor more disorderly? Would it make worse parents or children, husbands or wives, masters or servants, friends or neighbours? Or would it not make men more virtuous, and consequently more happy in every situation? It could not be criminal; it could not be detrimental. It could not be criminal, because it cannot be a crime to assent to such evidence, as has been able to convince the best and wisest of mankind; by

F 3
which,

which, if falſe, Providence muſt have permitted men to deceive each other, for the moſt beneficial ends, and which therefore it would be ſurely more meritorious to believe, from a diſpoſition of faith and charity, which believeth all things, than to reject with ſcorn from obſtinacy and ſelf conceit: It cannot be detrimental, becauſe if Chriſtianity is a fable, it is a fable, the belief of which is the only principle which can retain men in a ſteady and uniform courſe of virtue, piety, and devotion, or can ſupport them in the hour of diſtreſs, of ſickneſs, and of death. Whatever might be the operations of true deiſm on the minds of pagan philoſophers, that can now avail us nothing: for that light which once lightened the Gentiles, is now abſorbed in the brighter illumination of the goſpel; we can now form no rational ſyſtem of deiſm, but what muſt be borrowed from that ſource, and, as far as it reaches towards perfection, muſt be exactly the ſame; and therefore if we will not accept of Chriſtianity, we can have no religion at all.   Accordingly

cordingly we see, that those who fly from this, scarce ever stop at deism ; but hasten on with great alacrity to a total rejection of all religious and moral principles whatever.

If I have here demonstrated the divine origin of the Christian religion by an argument which cannot be confuted ; no others, however plausible or numerous, founded on probabilities, doubts, and conjectures, can ever disprove it, because if it is once shewn to be true, it cannot be false. But as many arguments of this kind have bewildered some candid and ingenuous minds, I shall here bestow a few lines on those which have the most weight, in order to wipe out, or at least to diminish their perplexing influence.

But here I must previously observe, that the most unsurmountable, as well as the most usual obstacle to our belief, arises from our passions, appetites, and interests ; for faith being an act of the will as much as of the understanding, we oftener disbelieve for want of inclination, than want of evidence. The first step towards thinking this revela-

tion

tion true, is our hopes that it is so; for whenever we much wish any proposition to be true, we are not far from believing it. It is certainly for the interest of all good men, that its authority should be well founded; and still more beneficial to the bad, if ever they intend to be better: because it is the only system either of reason or religion which can give them any assurance of pardon. The punishment of vice is a debt due to justice, which cannot be remitted without compensation: repentance can be no compensation; it may change a wicked man's dispositions, and prevent his offending for the future, but can lay no claim to pardon for what is past. If any one by profligacy and extravagance contracts a debt, repentance may make him wiser, and hinder him from running into further distresses, but can never pay off his old bonds; for which he must be ever accountable, unless they are discharged by himself, or some other in his stead: this very discharge Christianity alone holds forth on our repentance,

pentance, and, if true, will certainly perform : the truth of it therefore muſt ardently
be wiſhed for by all, except the wicked, who
are determined neither to repent or reform.
It is well worth every man's while, who
either is, or intends to be virtuous, to believe
Chriſtianity, if he can ; becauſe he will find
it the ſureſt preſervative againſt all vicious
habits and their attendant evils, the beſt re-
ſource under diſtreſſes and diſappointments,
ill health, and ill fortune, and the firmeſt ba-
ſis on which contemplation can reſt; and
without ſome, the human mind is never perfectly at eaſe. But if any one is attached
to a favourite pleaſure, or eagerly engaged in
worldly purſuits incompatible with the precepts of this religion, and he believes it, he
muſt either relinquiſh thoſe purſuits with
uneaſineſs, or perſiſt in them with remorſe
and diſſatisfaction, and therefore muſt com-
mence unbeliever in his own defence. With
ſuch I ſhall not diſpute, nor pretend to perſuade men by arguments to make themſelves miſerable : but to thoſe, who, not
afraid

afraid that this religion may be true, are really affected by such objections, I will offer the following answers, which, though short, will, I doubt not, be sufficient to shew them their weakness and futility.

In the first place, then, some have been so bold as to strike at the root of all revelation from God, by asserting, that it is incredible, because unnecessary, and unnecessary, because the reason which he has bestowed on mankind is sufficiently able to discover all the religious and moral duties which he requires of them, if they would but attend to her precepts, and be guided by her friendly admonitions. Mankind have undoubtedly at various times from the remotest ages received so much knowledge by divine communications, and have ever been so much inclined to impute it all to their own sufficiency, that it is now difficult to determine what human reason unassisted can effect : But to form a true judgment on this subject, let us turn our eyes to those remote regions of the globe, to which this supernatural assistance

fiftance has never yet extended, and we fhall
there fee men endued with fenfe and reafon
not inferior to our own, fo far from being
capable of forming fyftems of religion and
morality, that they are at this day totally
unable to make a nail or a hatchet : from
whence we may furely be convinced, that
reafon alone is fo far from being fufficient to
offer to mankind a perfect religion, that it
has never yet been able to lead them to
any degree of culture or civilization whatever. Thefe have uniformly flowed from
that great fountain of divine communication opened in the eaft, in the earlieft ages,
and thence been gradually diffufed in falu-
brious ftreams, throughout the various regions of the earth. Their rife and progrefs,
by furveying the hiftory of the world, may
eafily be traced backwards to their fource ;
and wherever thefe have not as yet been able
to penetrate, we there find the human fpecies not only void of all true religious
and moral fentiments, but not the leaft
emerged from their original ignorance and
barbarity ;

barbarity; which seems a demonstration, that although human reason is capable of progression in science, yet the first foundations must be laid by supernatural instructions: for surely no other probable cause can be assigned, why one part of mankind should have made such an amazing progress in religious, moral, metaphysical, and philosophical enquiries ; such wonderful improvements in policy, legislation, commerce, and manufactures, while the other part, formed with the same natural capacities, and divided only by seas and mountains, should remain, during the same number of ages, in a state little superior to brutes, without government, without laws or letters, and even without clothes and habitations ; murdering each other to satiate their revenge, and devouring each other to appease their hunger: I say no cause can be assigned for this amazing difference, except that the first have received information from those divine communications recorded in the scriptures, and the latter have never yet been favoured with such assistance.

affistance. This remarkable contraft seems an unanfwerable, though perhaps a new proof of the neceffity of revelation, and a folid refutation of all arguments againft it, drawn from the fufficiency of human reafon. And as reafon in her natural ftate is thus incapable of making any progrefs in knowledge; fo when furnifhed with materials by fupernatural aid, if left to the guidance of her own wild imaginations, fhe falls into more numerous and more grofs errors, than her own native ignorance could ever have fuggefted. There is then no abfurdity fo extravagant, which fhe is not ready to adopt: fhe has perfuaded fome, that there is no God; others, that there can be no future ftate: fhe has taught fome, that there is no difference between vice and virtue, and that to cut a man's throat and to relieve his neceffities are actions equally meritorious: fhe has convinced many, that they have no free-will, in oppofition to their own experience; fome, that there can be no fuch thing as foul, or fpirit, contrary to their own perceptions;

ceptions; and others, no such thing as matter or body, in contradiction to their senses.
By analysing all things she can shew, that
there is nothing in any thing; by perpetual
sifting she can reduce all existence to the invisible dust of scepticism; and by recurring
to first principles, prove to the satisfaction of
her followers, that there are no principles at
all. How far such a guide is to be depended
on in the important concerns of religion, and
morals, I leave to the judgment of every
considerate man to determine. This is certain, that human reason in its highest state
of cultivation amongst the philosophers of
Greece and Rome, was never able to form
a religion comparable to Christianity; nor
have all those sources of moral virtue, such
as truth, beauty, and the fitness of things,
which modern philosophers have endeavoured to substitute in its stead, ever been
effectual to produce good men, and have
themselves often been the productions of
some of the worst.

Others there are, who allow, that a revela-

5   tion

tion from God may be both neceſſary, and credible; but alledge, that the ſcriptures, that is the books of the Old and New Teſtament, cannot be that revelation; becauſe in them are to be found errors and inconſiſtencies, fabulous ſtories, falſe facts, and falſe philoſophy; which can never be derived from the fountain of all wiſdom and truth. To this I reply, that I readily acknowledge, that the ſcriptures are not revelations from God, but the hiſtory of them: The revelation itſelf is derived from God; but the hiſtory of it is the production of men, and therefore the truth of it is not in the leaſt affected by their fallibility, but depends on the internal evidence of its own ſupernatural excellence. If in theſe books ſuch a religion, as has been here deſcribed, actually exiſts, no ſeeming, or even real defects to be found in them can diſprove the divine origin of this religion, or invalidate my argument. Let us, for inſtance, grant that the Moſaic hiſtory of the creation was founded on the erroneous but popular prin-

ciples

ciples of those early ages, who imagined the earth to be a vast plain, and the celestial bodies no more than luminaries hung up in the concave firmament to enlighten it; will it from thence follow, that Moses could not be a proper instrument in the hands of Providence, to impart to the Jews a divine law, because he was not inspired with a foreknowledge of the Copernican and Newtonian systems? or that Christ must be an impostor, because Moses was not an astronomer? Let us also suppose, that the accounts of Christ's temptation in the wilderness, the devil's taking refuge in the herd of swine, with several other narrations in the New Testament, frequently ridiculed by unbelievers, were all but stories accommodated to the ignorance and superstitions of the times and countries in which they were written, or pious frauds intended to impress on vulgar minds a higher reverence of the power and sanctity of Christ; will this in the least impeach the excellence of his religion, or the authority of its founder? or is

Christianity

Christianity answerable for all the fables of which it may have been the innocent occasion? The want of this obvious distinction has much injured the Christian cause; because on this ground it has ever been most successfully attacked, and on this ground it is not easily to be defended: for if the records of this revelation are supposed to be the revelation itself, the least defect discovered in them must be fatal to the whole. What has led many to overlook this distinction, is that common phrase, that the scriptures are the word of God; and in one sense they certainly are; that is, they are the sacred repository of all the revelations, dispensations, promises, and precepts, which God has vouchsafed to communicate to mankind; but by this expression we are not to understand, that every part of this voluminous collection of historical, poetical, prophetical, theological, and moral writings, which we call the Bible, was dictated by the immediate influence of divine inspiration: the authors of these books pretend to no such infallibility, and if they claim it not for themselves, who has the authority to claim it for them? Christ required no such belief from those who were willing to be his disciples. He says, " He that believeth on " me, hath everlasting life*;" but where does he say, He that believeth not every word contained in the Old Testament, which was then extant, or every word in the New Testament, which was to be wrote for the instruction of future generations, hath not everlasting life? There are innumerable occurrences related in the scriptures, some of greater, some of less, and some of no importance at all; the truth of which we can have no reason to question, but the belief of them is surely not essential to the faith of a Christian: I have no doubt but that St. Paul was shipwrecked, and that he left his cloak and his parchments at Troas; but the belief of these facts makes no part of Christianity, nor is the truth of them any proof of its authority. It proves only that this apostle could

* John vi. 47.

not

not in common life be under the perpetual influence of infallible infpiration; for, had he been fo, he would not have put to fea before a ftorm, nor have forgot his cloak. Thefe writers were undoubtedly directed by fupernatural influence in all things neceffary to the great work, which they were appointed to perform: At particular times, and on particular occafions, they were enabled to utter prophecies, to fpeak languages, and to work miracles; but in all other circumftances, they feem to have been left to the direction of their own underftandings, like other men. In the fciences of hiftory, geography, aftronomy, and philofophy, they appear to have been no better inftructed than others, and therefore were not lefs liable to be mifled by the errors and prejudices of the times and countries in which they lived. They related facts like honeft men, to the beft of their knowledge or information, and they recorded the divine leffons of their mafter with the utmoft fidelity; but they pretended to no infallibility, for they fometimes differed

G 2   in

in their relations, and they fometimes dif-
agreed in their fentiments. All which
proves only, that they did not act, or write,
in a combination to deceive, but not in the
leaft impeaches the truth of the revelation
which they publifhed; which depends not
on any external evidence whatever: for I
will venture to affirm, that if any one could
prove, what is impoffible to be proved, becaufe it is not true, that there are errors in
geography, chronology, and philofophy, in
every page of the Bible; that the prophecies
therein delivered are all but fortunate gueffes,
or artful applications, and the miracles there
recorded no better than legendary tales: if
any one could fhew, that thefe books were
never written by their pretended authors,
but were pofterior impofitions on illiterate
and credulous ages: all thefe wonderful difcoveries would prove no more than this,
tht God, for reafons to us unknown, had
thought proper to permit a revelation by
him communicated to mankind, to be mixed
with their ignorance, and corrupted by their
                                        frauds

frauds from its earlieſt infancy, in the ſame manner in which he has viſibly permitted it to be mixed, and corrupted from that period to the preſent hour. If in theſe books a religion ſuperior to all human imagination actually exiſts, it is of no conſequence to the proof of its divine origin, by what means it was there introduced, or with what human errors and imperfections it is blended. A diamond, though found in a bed of mud, is ſtill a diamond, nor can the dirt, which ſurrounds it, depreciate its value or deſtroy its luſtre.

To ſome ſpeculative and refined obſervers, it has appeared incredible, that a wiſe and benevolent Creator ſhould have conſtituted a world upon one plan, and a religion for it on another; that is, that he ſhould have revealed a religion to mankind, which not only contradicts the principal paſſions and inclinations which he has implanted in their natures, but is incompatible with the whole œconomy of that world which he has created, and in which he has thought proper to

G 3   place

place them. This, fay they, with regard to
the Chriftian is apparently the cafe: the
love of power, riches, honour, and fame, are
the great incitements to generous and magnanimous actions; yet by this inftitution are
all thefe depreciated and difcouraged. Government is effential to the nature of man,
and cannot be managed without certain degrees of violence, corruption, and impofi-
tion; yet are all thefe ftrictly forbid. Nations cannot fubfift without wars, nor war
be carried on without rapine, defolation, and
murder; yet are thefe prohibited under the
fevereft threats. The non-refiftance of evil
muft fubject individuals to continual op-
preffions, and leave nations a defencelefs prey
to their enemies; yet is this recommended.
Perpetual patience under infults and injuries muft every day provoke new infults and
new injuries; yet is this enjoined. A neglect of all we eat and drink and wear, muft
put an end to all commerce, manufactures,
and induftry; yet is this required. In fhort,
were thefe precepts univerfally obeyed, the
disposition

difpofition of all human affairs muft be entirely changed, and the bufinefs of the
world, conftituted as it now is, could not go
on. To all this I anfwer, that fuch indeed is
the Chriftian revelation, though fome of its
advocates may perhaps be unwilling to own
it, and fuch it is conftantly declared to be by
him who gave it, as well as by thofe who
publifhed it under his immediate direction:
To thefe he fays, " If ye were of the world,
" the world would love his own; but be-
" caufe ye are not of the world, but I have
" chofen you out of the world, therefore the
" world hateth you *." To the Jews he
declares, " Ye are of this world; I am not
" of this world †." St. Paul writes to the
Romans, " Be not conformed to this
" world ‡;" and to the Corinthians, " We
" fpeak not the wifdom of this world §."
St. James fays, " Know ye not, that the
" friendfhip of the world is enmity with
" God ? whofoever therefore will be a

* John xv. 19.   † John viii. 23.
‡ Rom. xii. 2.   § 1 Cor. ii. 6.

" friend

" friend of the world is the enemy of
" God *." This irreconcileable difagree-
ment between Chriftianity and the world is
announced in numberlefs other places in the
New Teftament, and indeed by the whole
tenour of thofe writings. Thefe are plain
declarations, which, in fpite of all the eva-
fions of thofe good managers, who choofe to
take a little of this world in their way to
heaven, ftand fixed and immoveable againft
all their arguments drawn from public benefit and pretended neceffity, and muft ever
forbid any reconciliation between the purfuits of this world and the Chriftian inftitution: but they who reject it on this account,
enter not into the fublime fpirit of this religion, which is not a code of precife laws defigned for the well-ordering fociety, adapted
to the ends of worldly convenience, and
amenable to the tribunal of human pru-
dence; but a divine leffon of purity and
perfection, fo far fuperior to the low con-
fiderations of conqueft, government, and

* Jam. iv. 4.

commerce,

commerce, that it takes no more notice of them, than of the battles of game-cocks, the policy of bees, or the induſtry of ants : they recollect not what is the firſt and principal object of this inſtitution ; that this is **not**, as has been often repeated, to make us hap-py, or even virtuous in the preſent life, for the ſake of augmenting our happineſs here ; but to conduct us through a ſtate of dangers and ſufferings, of ſin and temptation, in ſuch a manner as to qualify us for the enjoyment of happineſs hereafter. All other inſtitu-tions of religion and morals were made for the world, but the characteriſtic of this is to be againſt it ; and therefore the merits of Chriſtian doctrines are not to be weighed in the ſcales of public utility, like thoſe of mo-ral precepts, becauſe worldly utility is not their end. If Chriſt and his apoſtles had pretended, that the religion which they preached would advance the power, wealth, and proſperity of nations, or of men, they would have deſerved but little credit ; but they conſtantly profeſs the contrary, and

5   every

every where declare, that their religion is adverse to the world, and all its pursuits. Christ says, speaking of his disciples, " They " are not of the world, even as I am not of " the world *." It can therefore be no imputation on this religion, or on any of its precepts, that they tend not to an end which their author professedly disclaims : nor can it surely be deemed a defect, that it is adverse to the vain pursuits of this world ; for so are reason, wisdom, and experience ; they all teach us the same lesson, they all demonstrate to us every day, that these are begun on false hopes, carried on with disquietude, and end in disappointment. This professed incompatibility with the little, wretched, and iniquitous business of the world, is therefore so far from being a defect in this religion, that, was there no other proof of its divine origin, this alone, I think, would be abundantly sufficient. The great plan and benevolent design of this dispensation is plainly this; to enlighten the minds, purify the reli-

* John xvii. 16.

gion,

gion, and amend the morals of mankind in general, and to select the most meritorious of them to be succeffively tranfplanted into the kingdom of heaven: which gracious offer is impartially tendered to all, who by perfeverance in meeknefs, patience, piety, charity, and a detachment from the world, are willing to qualify themfelves for this holy and happy fociety. Was this univerfally accepted, and did every man obferve ftrictly every precept of the gofpel, the face of human affairs and the œconomy of the world would indeed be greatly changed but furely they would be changed for the better; and we fhould enjoy much more happinefs, even here, than at prefent: for we muft not forget, that evils are by it forbid as well as refiftance; injuries, as well as revenge; all unwillingnefs to diffufe the enjoyments of life, as well as folicitude to acquire them; all obftacles to ambition, as well as ambition itfelf; and therefore all contentions for power and intereft would be at an end; and the world would go on much more happily
than

than it now does. But this univerſal acceptance of ſuch an offer was never expected
from ſo depraved and imperfect a creature as
man, and therefore could never have been any
part of the deſign: for it was foreknown
and foretold by him who made it, that few,
very few would accept it on theſe terms.
He ſays, " Strait is the gate, and narrow is
" the way which leadeth into life, and few
" there be that find it *." Accordingly we
ſee, that very few are prevailed on, by the
hopes of future happineſs, to relinquiſh the
purſuits of preſent pleaſures or intereſts, and
therefore theſe purſuits are little interrupted
by the ſeceſſion of ſo inconſiderable a number. As the natural world ſubſiſts by the
ſtruggles of the ſame elements, ſo does the
moral by the contentions of the ſame paſſions, as from the beginning: the generality of mankind are actuated by the ſame
motives, fight, ſcuffle, and ſcramble for
power, riches, and pleaſures with the ſame
eagerneſs: all occupations and profeſſions

* Matt. vii. 4.

are

are exercised with the same alacrity, and
there are soldiers, lawyers, statesmen, patriots, and politicians, just as if Christianity
had never existed. Thus we see this wonderful dispensation has answered all the
purposes for which it was intended : it has
enlightened the minds, purified the religion,
and amended the morals of mankind ; and,
without subverting the constitution, policy,
or business of the world, opened a gate,
though a strait one, through which all, who
are wise enough to choose it, and good
enough to be fit for it, may find an entrance
into the kingdom of heaven.

Others have said, that if this revelation had
really been from God, his infinite power and
goodness could never have suffered it to
have been so soon perverted from its original purity, to have continued in a state of
corruption through the course of so many
ages, and at last to have proved so ineffectual to the reformation of mankind. To
these I answer, that all this, on examination,
will be found inevitable, from the nature of
all

all revelations communicated to so imperfect a creature as man, and from circumstances peculiar to the rise and progress of
the Christian in particular : for when this was
first preached to the gentile nations, though
they were not able to withstand the force of
its evidence, and therefore received it ; yet
they could not be prevailed on to relinquish
their old superstitions, and former opinions,
but chose rather to incorporate them with it :
by which means it was necessarily mixed with
their ignorance, and their learning; by both
which it was equally injured. The people
defaced its worship by blending it with their
idolatrous ceremonies, and the philosophers
corrupted its doctrines by weaving them up
with the notions of the Gnostics, Mystics,
and Manichæans, the prevailing systems of
those times. By degrees its irresistible excellence gained over princes, potentates, and
conquerors to its interests, and it was sup-
ported by their patronage : but that patronage soon engaged it in their policies and
contests, and destroyed that excellence by
which

which it had been acquired. At length the meek and humble professors of the gospel enslaved these princes, and conquered these conquerors their patrons, and erected for themselves such a stupendous fabric of wealth and power, as the world had never seen: they then propagated their religion by the same methods, by which it had been perfecuted; nations were converted by fire and sword, and the vanquished were baptized with daggers at their throats. All these events we see proceed from a chain of causes and consequences, which could not have been broken without changing the established course of things by a constant series of miracles, or a total alteration of human nature: whilst that continues as it is, the purest religion must be corrupted by a conjunction with power and riches, and it will also then appear to be much more corrupted than it really is; because many are inclined to think, that every deviation from its primitive state is a corruption. Christianity was at first preached by the poor and mean, in holes

and

and caverns, under the iron rod of persecution, and therefore many absurdly conclude,
that any degree of wealth or power in its ministers, or of magnificence in its worship, are
corruptions inconsistent with the genuine simplicity of its original state : they are offended, that modern bishops should possess
titles, palaces, revenues, and coaches, when
it is notorious, that their predecessors the
apostles were despicable wanderers, without
houses or money, and walked on foot. The
apostles indeed lived in a state of poverty
and persecution attendant on their particular
situation, and the work which they had undertaken ; this was their misfortune, but no
part of their religion, and therefore it can
be no more incumbent on their successors to
imitate their poverty and meanness, than to
be whipped, imprisoned, and put to death,
in compliance with their example. These
are all but the suggestions of envy and malevolence, but no objections to these fortunate
alterations in Christianity and its professors ;
which,

which, if not abused to the purposes of tyranny and superstition, are in fact no more than the necessary and proper effects of its more prosperous situation. When a poor man grows rich, or a servant becomes a master, they should take care that their exaltation prompts them not to be unjust or insolent; but surely it is not requisite or right, that their behaviour and mode of living should be exactly the same, when their situation is altered. How far this institution has been effectual to the reformation of mankind, it is not easy now to ascertain, because the enormities which prevailed before the appearance of it are by time so far removed from our sight, that they are scarcely visible; but those of the most gigantic size still remain in the records of history, as monuments of the rest: Wars in those ages were carried on with a ferocity and cruelty unknown to the present: whole cities and nations were extirpated by fire and sword; and thousands of the vanquished were crucified and impaled for having endeavoured only to defend themselves and their country. The lives of new-born infants were then intirely at the disposal of their parents, who were at liberty to bring them up, or to expose them to perish by cold and hunger, or to be devoured by birds and beasts; and this was frequently practised without punishment, and even without censure. Gladiators were employed by hundreds to cut one another to pieces in public theatres for the diversion of the most polite assemblies; and though these combatants at first consisted of criminals only, by degrees men of the highest rank, and even ladies of the most illustrious families, enrolled themselves in this honourable list. On many occasions human sacrifices were ordained; and at the funerals of rich and eminent persons, great numbers of their slaves were murdered as victims pleasing to their departed spirits. The most infamous obscenities were made part of their religious worship, and the most unnatural lusts publickly avowed, and celebrated by their most admired poets. At the approach of Christianity

tianity all thefe horrid abominations vanifh-
ed; and amongft thofe who firft embraced
it, fcarce a fingle vice was to be found: to
fuch an amazing degree of piety, charity,
temperance, patience, and refignation were
the primitive converts exalted, that they feem
literally to have been regenerated, and purified from all the imperfections of human nature; and to have purfued fuch a conftant
and uniform courfe of devotion, innocence,
and virtue, as, in the prefent times, it is almoft as difficult for us to conceive as to imitate. If it is afked, why fhould not the
belief of the fame religion now produce the
fame effects? the anfwer is fhort, becaufe it
is not believed: The moft fovereign medicine can perform no cure, if the patient will
not be perfuaded to take it. Yet notwithftanding all impediments, it has certainly
done a great deal towards diminifhing the
vices and correcting the difpofitions of
mankind; and was it univerfally adopted in
belief and practice, would totally eradicate
both fin and punifhment. But this was ne-

H 2

ver expected, or designed, or possible, because, if their existence did not arise from
some necessity to us unknown, they never
would have been permitted to exist at all;
and therefore they can no more be extirpated, than they could have been prevented:
for this would certainly be incompatible with
the frame and constitution of this world, and
in all probability with that of another. And
this, I think, well accounts for that reserve
and obscurity with which this religion was
at first promulgated, and that want of irresistible evidence of its truth, by which it
might possibly have been enforced. Christ
says to his disciples, "To you it is given to
" know the mystery of the kingdom of God;
" but unto them that are without, all these
" things are done in parables; that seeing
" they may see, and not perceive, and hear-
" ing they may hear, and not understand;
" lest at any time they should be converted,
" and their sins should be forgiven them *."
That is, to you by peculiar favour it is given

* Mark iv. 11, 12.

to know and understand the doctrines of my religion, and by that means to qualify your-selves for the kingdom of heaven; but to the multitude without, that is to all man-kind in general, this indulgence cannot be extended; because that all men should be exempted from sin and punishment is utterly repugnant to the universal system, and that constitution of things, which infinite wisdom has thought proper to adopt.

Objections have likewise been raised to the divine authority of this religion from the incredibility of some of its doctrines, parti-cularly of those concerning the Trinity, and atonement for sin by the sufferings and death of Christ; the one contradicting all the principles of human reason, and the other all our ideas of divine justice. To these ob-jections I shall only say, that no arguments founded on principles, which we cannot comprehend, can possibly disprove a pro-position already proved on principles which we do understand; and therefore that on this subject they ought not to be attended to:

H 3　　　　　　That

That three Beings should be one Being, is a proposition which certainly contradicts reason, that is, *our* reason; but it does not from thence follow, that it cannot be true; for there are many propositions which contradict our reason, and yet are demonstrably true: one is the very first principle of all religion, the being of a God; for that any thing should exist without a cause, or that any thing should be the cause of its own existence, are propositions equally contradictory to our reason; yet one of them must be true, or nothing could ever have existed: in like manner the over-ruling grace of the Creator, and the free-will of his creatures, his certain fore-knowledge of future events, and the uncertain contingency of those events, are to our apprehensions absolute contradictions to each other; and yet the truth of every one of these is demonstrable from Scripture, reason, and experience. All these difficulties arise from our imagining, that the mode of existence of all Beings must be similar to our own; that is, that they

must

muſt all exiſt in time, and ſpace; and hence
proceeds our embarraſſment on this ſubjeƈt.
We know, that no two Beings, with whoſe
mode of exiſtence we are acquainted, can exiſt
in the ſame point of time, in the ſame point of
ſpace, and that therefore they cannot be one:
but how far Beings, whoſe mode of exiſtence
bears no relation to time or ſpace, may be
united, we cannot comprehend: and therefore
the poſſibility of ſuch an union we cannot poſi-
tively deny. In like manner our reaſon informs
us, that the puniſhment of the innocent, inſtead of the guilty, is diametrically oppoſite
to juſtice, reƈtitude, and all pretenſions to
utility; but we ſhould alſo remember, that
the ſhort line of our reaſon cannot reach to
the bottom of this queſtion: it cannot inform us, by what means either guilt or puniſhment ever gained a place in the works
of a Creator infinitely good and powerful,
whoſe goodneſs muſt have induced him, and
whoſe power muſt have enabled him, to exclude them: It cannot aſſure us, that ſome
ſufferings of individuals are not neceſſary to

H 4　　　　　the

the happiness and well-being of the whole:
It cannot convince us, that they do not actually arise from this necessity, or that, for this
cause, they may not be required of us, and
levied like a tax for the public benefit; or
that this tax may not be paid by one Being,
as well as another; and therefore, if voluntarily offered, be justly accepted from the
innocent instead of the guilty. Of all these
circumstances we are totally ignorant; nor
can our reason afford us any information,
and therefore we are not able to assert, that
this measure is contrary to justice, or void
of utility: for, unless we could first resolve
that great question, Whence came evil? we
can decide nothing on the dispensations of
Providence; because they must necessarily
be connected with that undiscoverable principle; and, as we know not the root of the
disease, we cannot judge of what is, or is
not, a proper and effectual remedy. It is
remarkable, that, notwithstanding all the
seeming absurdities of this doctrine, there is
one circumstance much in its favour; which
is,

is, that it has been univerſally adopted in
all ages, as far as hiſtory can carry us back
in our inquiries to the earlieſt times ; in
which we find all nations, civilized and bar-
barous, however differing in all other religious opinions, agreeing alone in the ex-
pediency of appeaſing their offended Deities
by ſacrifices, that is, by the vicarious ſufferings of men or other animals. This notion
could never have been derived from reaſon,
becauſe it directly contradicts it ; nor from
ignorance, becauſe ignorance could never
have contrived ſo unaccountable an expedient, nor have been uniform in all ages and
countries in any opinion whatſoever ; nor
from the artifice of kings or prieſts, in order
to acquire dominion over the people, becauſe it ſeems not adapted to this end ; and
we find it implanted in the minds of the moſt
remote ſavages at this day diſcovered, who
have neither kings or prieſts, artifice or dominion, amongſt them. It muſt therefore be
derived from natural inſtinct or ſupernatural
revelation, both which are equally the operations

rations of divine power. If it is further urged, that however true thefe doctrines may be, yet it muft be inconfiftent with the juftice and goodnefs of the Creator, to require from his creatures the belief of propofitions which contradict, or are above the reach of that reafon, which he has thought proper to beftow upon them. To this I anfwer, that genuine Chriftianity requires no fuch belief: It has difcovered to us many important truths, with which we were before intirely unacquainted; and amongft them are thefe: that three Beings are fome way united in the divine effence; and that God will accept of the fufferings of Chrift as an atonement for the fins of mankind. Thefe, confidered as declarations of facts only, neither contradict, or are above the reach of human reafon: The firft is a propofition as plain, as that three equilateral lines compofe one triangle; the other is as intelligible, as that one man fhould difcharge the debts of another. In what manner this union is formed, or why God accepts thefe vicarious punifhments,

nifhments, or to what purpofes they may be
fubfervient, it informs us not, becaufe no information could enable us to comprehend
thefe myfteries; and therefore it does not require that we fhould know or believe any thing
about them. The truth of thefe doctrines
muft reft intirely on the authority of thofe
who taught them; but then we fhould reflect
that thofe were the fame perfons who taught
us a fyftem of religion more fublime, and of
ethics more perfect, than any which our faculties were ever able to difcover, but which
when difcovered are exactly confonant to
our reafon; and that therefore we fhould
not haftily reject thofe informations which
they have vouchfafed to give us, of which
our reafon is not a competent judge. If an
able mathematician proves to us the truth of
feveral propofitions by demonftrations which
we underftand, we hefitate not on his authority to affent to others, the procefs of whofe
proofs we are not able to follow: why therefore fhould we refufe that credit to Chrift
and

and his Apostles, which we think reasonable to give to one another?

Many have objected to the whole scheme of this revelation, as partial, fluctuating, indeterminate, unjust, and unworthy of an omniscient and omnipotent author, who cannot be supposed to have favoured particular persons, countries, and times, with this divine communication, while others no less meritorious have been altogether excluded from its benefits; nor to have changed and counteracted his own designs; that is, to have formed mankind able and disposed to render themselves miserable by their own wickedness, and then to have contrived so strange an expedient to restore them to that happiness which they need never have been permitted to forfeit; and this to be brought about by the unnecessary interposition of a mediator. To all this I shall only say, that however unaccountable this may appear to us, who see but as small a part of the Christian, as of the universal plan of creation, they are both in regard to all these circumstances exactly ana-

5   logous

logous to each other. In all the difpenfations of Providence, with which we are acquainted, benefits are diftributed in a fimilar
manner ; health and ftrength, fenfe and fcience, wealth and power, are all beftowed on
individuals and communities in different degrees and at different times. The whole
œconomy of this world confifts of evils and
remedies ; and thefe for the moft part ad-
miniftered by the inftrumentality of intermediate agents. God has permitted us to plunge
ourfelves into poverty, diftrefs, and mifery,
by our own vices, and has afforded us the advice, inftructions, and examples of others, to
deter or extricate us from thefe calamities.
He has formed us fubject to innumerable
difeafes, and he has beftowed on us a variety
of remedies. He has made us liable to
hunger, thirft, and nakednefs, and he fup-
plies us with food, drink, and clothing, ufu-
fually by the adminiftration of others. He has
created poifons, and he has provided antidotes.
He has ordained the winter's cold to cure the
peftilential heats of the fummer, and the fummer's funfhine to dry up the inundations of the
winter.

winter. Why the conftitution of nature is fo formed, why all the vifible difpenfations of Providence are fuch, and why fuch is the Chriftian difpenfation alfo, we know not, nor have faculties to comprehend. God might certainly have made the material world a fyftem of perfect beauty and regularity, without evils, and without remedies; and the Chriftian difpenfation a fcheme only of moral virtue, productive of happinefs, without the intervention of any atonement or mediation. He might have exempted our bodies from all difeafes, and our minds from all depravity, and we fhould then have ftood in no need of medicines to reftore us to health, or expedients to reconcile us to his favour. It feems indeed to our ignorance, that this would have been more confiftent with juftice and reafon; but his infinite wifdom has decided in another manner, and formed the fyftems both of Nature and Chriftianity on other principles; and thefe fo exactly fimilar, that we have caufe to conclude that they both muft proceed

ceed from the same source of divine power
and wisdom, however inconsistent with our
reason they may appear. Reason is undoubtedly our surest guide in all matters,
which lie within the narrow circle of her in-
telligence : On the subject of revelation her
province is only to examine into its authority ; and when that is once proved, she has
no more to do, but to acquiesce in its doctrines ; and therefore is never so ill employed, as when she pretends to accommodate
them to her own ideas of rectitude and truth.
God, says this self-sufficient teacher, is perfectly wise, just, and good ; and what is the
inference ? That all his dispensations must
be conformable to our notions of perfect wisdom, justice, and goodness : but it should
first be proved, that man is as perfect, and as
wise as his Creator, or this consequence will
by no means follow ; but rather the reverse,
that is, that the dispensations of a perfect and
all-wise Being must probably appear unrea-
sonable, and perhaps unjust, to a Being imperfect and ignorant ; and therefore their
seeming

feeming impoffibility may be a mark of their truth, and in fome meafure juftify that pious rant of a mad enthufiaft, " Credo, quia im-" poffibile." Nor is it the leaft furprifing, that we are not able to underftand the fpiritual difpenfations of the Almighty, when his material works are to us no lefs incomprehenfible; our reafon can afford us no infight into thofe great properties of matter, gravitation, attraction, elafticity, and electricity, nor even into the effence of matter itfelf: Can reafon teach us now the fun's luminous orb can fill a circle, whofe diameter contains many millions of miles, with a conftant inundation of fucceffive rays, during thoufands of years, without any perceivable diminution of that body, from whence they are continually poured, or any augmentation of thofe bodies on which they fall, and by which they are conftantly abforbed? Can reafon tell us how thofe rays, darted with a velocity greater than that of a cannon-ball, can ftrike the tendereft organs of the human frame without inflicting any degree of pain,

or

or by what means this percussion only can convey the forms of distant objects to an immaterial mind ? or how any union can be formed between material and immaterial essences, or how the wounds of the body can give pain to the soul, or the anxiety of the soul can emaciate and destroy the body ? That all these things are so, we have visible and indisputable demonstration ; but how they can be so, is to us as incomprehensible, as the most abstruse mysteries of revelation can possibly be. In short, we see so small a part of the great whole ; we know so little of the relation, which the present life bears to pre-existent and future states; we can conceive so little of the nature of God, and his attributes, or mode of existence ; we can comprehend so little of the material, and so much less of the moral plan on which the universe is constituted, or on what principle it proceeds, that, if a revelation from such a being, on such subjects, was in every part familiar to our understandings, and consonant to our reason, we should have great cause to suspect its divine authority; and therefore, had this revelation been less incomprehensible, it would certainly have been more incredible.

But I shall not enter further into the consideration of these abstruse and difficult speculations, because the discussion of them would render this short essay too tedious and laborious a task for the perusal of them, for whom it was principally intended; which are all those busy or idle persons, whose time and thoughts are wholly engrossed by the pursuits of business or pleasure, ambition or luxury, who know nothing of this religion, except what they have accidentally picked up by desultory conversation or superficial reading, and have thence determined with themselves, that a pretended revelation, founded on so strange and improbable a story, so contradictory to reason, so adverse to the world and all its occupations, so incredible in its doctrines, and in its precepts so impracticable, can be nothing more than the imposition of priestcraft upon ignorant

5   and

and illiterate ages, and artfully continued as
an engine well adapted to awe and govern
the superstitious vulgar. To talk to such
about the Christian religion, is to converse
with the deaf concerning music, or with the
blind on the beauties of painting: they
want all ideas relative to the subject, and
therefore can never be made to comprehend
it: to enable them to do this, their minds
must be formed for these conceptions by
contemplation, retirement, and abstraction
from business and dissipation; by ill-health,
disappointments, and distresses; and possibly
by divine interposition, or by enthusiasm,
which is usually mistaken for it. Without
some of these preparatory aids, together with
a competent degree of learning and application, it is impossible that they can think or
know, understand or believe, any thing
about it. If they profess to believe, they
deceive others; if they fancy that they believe, they deceive themselves. I am ready
to acknowledge, that these gentlemen, as far
as their information reaches, are perfectly in

I 2

the

the right ; and if they are endued with good underſtandings, which have been intirely devoted to the buſineſs or amuſements of the world, they can paſs no other judgment, and muſt revolt from the hiſtory and doctrines of this religion. " The preaching Chriſt " crucified was to the Jews a ſtumbling- " block, and to the Greeks fooliſhneſs * ;" and ſo it muſt appear to all, who, like them, judge from eſtabliſhed prejudices, falſe learning, and ſuperficial knowledge; for thoſe who are quite unable to follow the chain of its prophecy, to ſee the beauty and juſtneſs of its moral precepts, and to enter into the wonders of its diſpenſations, can form no other idea of this revelation, but that of a confuſed rhapſody of fictions and abſurdities.

If it is aſked, Was Chriſtianity then intended only for learned divines and profound philoſophers ? I anſwer, No : it was at firſt preached by the illiterate, and received by the ignorant; and to ſuch are the

* 1 Cor. i. 26.

practical;

practical, which are the moft neceffary parts of it fufficiently intelligible : but the proofs of its authority undoubtedly are not, becaufe thefe muft be chiefly drawn from other parts, of a fpeculative nature, opening to our inquiries inexhauftible difcoveries concerning the nature, attributes, and difpenfations of God, which cannot be underftood without fome learning and much attention. From thefe the generality of mankind muft neceffarily be excluded, and muft therefore truft to others for the grounds of their belief, if they believe at all. And hence perhaps it is, that faith, or eafinefs of belief, is fo frequently and fo ftrongly recommended in the gofpel ; becaufe if men require proofs, of which they themfelves are incapable, and thofe who have no knowledge on this important fubject will not place fome confidence in thofe who have ; the illiterate and unattentive muft ever continue in a ftate of unbelief : but then all fuch fhould remember, that in all fciences, even in mathematics themfelves, there are many propofitions, which on a

I 3   curfory

curſory view appear to the moſt acute underſtandings, uninſtructed in that ſcience, to
be impoſſible to be true, which yet on a
cloſer examination are found to be truths
capable of the ſtricteſt demonſtration; and
that therefore, in diſquiſitions on which we
cannot determine without much learned in-
veſtigation, reaſon uninformed is by no
means to be depended on ; and from hence
they ought ſurely to conclude, that it may
be at leaſt as poſſible for them to be miſ-
taken in diſbelieving this revelation, who
know nothing of the matter, as for thoſe
great maſters of reaſon and erudition, Gro-
tius, Bacon, Newton, Boyle, Locke, Addi-
ſon, and Lyttelton, to be deceived in their
belief : a belief, to which they firmly adhered
after the moſt diligent and learned reſearches
into the authenticity of its records, the completion of the prophecies, the ſublimity of
its doctrines, the purity of its precepts, and
the arguments of its adverſaries; a belief,
which they have teſtified to the world by
their writings, without any other motive,
than

than their regard for truth and the benefit of mankind. Should the few foregoing pages add but one mite to the treasures with which these learned writers have enriched the world; if they should be so fortunate as to persuade any of these minute philosophers to place some confidence in these great opinions, and to distrust their own; if they should be able to convince them, that notwithstanding all unfavourable appearances, Christianity may not be altogether artifice and error; if they should prevail on them to examine it with some attention, or, if that is too much trouble, not to reject it without any examination at all; the purpose of this little work will be sufficiently answered. Had the arguments herein used, and the new hints here flung out, been more largely discussed, it might easily have been extended to a more considerable bulk; but then the busy would not have had leisure, nor the idle inclination to have read it. Should it ever have the honour to be admitted into such good

I 4

company,

company, they will immediately, I know, determine, that it muſt be the work of ſome enthuſiaſt or methodiſt, ſome beggar, or ſome madman. I ſhall therefore beg leave to aſſure them, that the author is very far removed from all theſe characters: that he once perhaps believed as little as themſelves; but having ſome leiſure and more curioſity, he employed them both in reſolving a queſtion which ſeemed to him of ſome importance—Whether Chriſtianity was really an impoſture founded on an abſurd, incredible, and obſolete fable, as many ſuppoſe it? Or whether it is, what it pretends to be, a revelation communicated to mankind by the interpoſition of ſupernatural power? On a candid enquiry, he ſoon found, that the firſt was an abſolute impoſſibility, and that its pretenſions to the latter were founded on the moſt ſolid grounds: in the further purſuit of his examination, he perceived, at every ſtep, new lights ariſing, and ſome of the brighteſt from parts of it the moſt obſcure, but productive of the cleareſt proofs, becauſe

equally

equally beyond the power of human artifice to invent, and human reason to difcover. Thefe arguments, which have convinced him of the divine origin of this religion, he has here put together in as clear and concife a manner as he was able, thinking they might have the fame effect upon others, and being of opinion, that if there were a few more true Chriftians in the world, it would be beneficial to themfelves, and by no means detrimental to the public.

SHORT AND CURSORY

OBSERVATIONS

ON

SEVERAL PASSAGES

IN THE

NEW TESTAMENT.

CURSORY OBSERVATIONS.

MATT. V. 3.

Μακαριοι οἱ πλωχοι τῳ πνευμαϕι, ὁτι αὐτων ἐϛιν ἡ βασιλεια των ἐρανων.

Bleſſed are the poor in ſpirit, for theirs is the kingdom of heaven.

IN this declaration of Chriſt, two queſtions offer themſelves to our conſideration: 1ſt, Who are the poor in ſpirit ?—And 2d, What is the kingdom of heaven ?

By the poor in ſpirit are here meant, thoſe who, by their natural diſpoſitions, are meek, quiet, teachable, and ſubmiſſive; or thoſe who, by reflection and cultivation, have rendered their diſpoſitions ſuch, and have eradicated from their hearts pride, envy, and ambition, thoſe high-ſpirited paſſions, ſo deſtructive of the happineſs of ſociety, as well as of their own. What portion of mankind

comes

comes under this defcription is known only to the fearcher of all hearts; but we may reafonably conclude, that neither heroes, conquerors, or any of thofe whom the world dignifies with the titles of great men, can be of the number.

By the kingdom of heaven is here to be underftood, that celeftial community of the fpirits* of juft men made perfeét, over which God more immediately prefides, and which is therefore fometimes called the kingdom of God; in which there are no wars, faétions, ftruggles, or contentions, but all is benevolence, peace, concord, and fubordination: a kingdom frequently hung out to our view in the New Teftament, of which we are promifed to be made fubjeéts in a future life, provided we fhall be properly qualified for it by our behaviour in the prefent.

To feleét the moft excellent of mankind, and to qualify them for admiffion into this holy and happy fociety, feems to be the chief objeét of the Chriftian difpenfation.

* Heb. xii. 23.

What

What that qualification muſt be, we are ſufficiently informed by the author of it— Calling to him little children, he ſays, " Of " ſuch is the kingdom of God ;" and again, " Verily I ſay unto you, Whoſoever ſhall not " receive the kingdom of God as a little child, " he ſhall not enter therein *." It is alſo evident from the nature of this community, that none but the poor in ſpirit can be admitted ; becauſe, were the proud, factious, turbulent, and ambitious to find entrance, they would immediately deſtroy that tranquillity and happineſs with which it is bleſſed ; and this kingdom, though not of this world, would ſoon become exactly ſimilar to thoſe which are.

It is ſaid, " Many are called, but few are " choſen ;" but we are not therefore to conclude, that all who are not choſen are to be conſigned to a ſtate of miſery ; many who are deficient in this neceſſary qualification, and therefore inadmiſſible into this ſtate of purity and perfection, may deſerve no greater puniſh-

* Mark x. 14, 15.

ment

ment than the loss of so inestimable an acquisition; and some perhaps may have virtues which may entitle them to rewards of an inferior kind. Mankind are by no means divisible into two classes only—the righteous and the wicked. We find them indeed so divided in many passages of the New Testament, all which must be understood but as general declarations, that the righteous shall be rewarded, and the wicked punished, in a future life; but cannot be applied to individuals, because in fact no such line of distinction can be drawn between them. The generality of mankind are compleatly neither the one or the other: none are so good as to be guilty of no crimes, and few so bad as to be possessed of no virtues; and in most men they are intermixed, though in very different proportions. The justice of Providence must have prepared many intermediate states of happiness and misery, in which every individual will receive reward or punishment in exact proportion to his merits. Astronomy has opened to our view

innumerable

innumerable worlds, fome of which are probably happier, and fome more miferable
than this which we at prefent inhabit ; in
them there is ample room for the difplay of
the divine juftice and benevolence, as in
fome of them fuch a fituation may be allotted to every one as his conduct has deferved.

MATT. V. 5.

Μακαριοι οἱ πραεις, ὁτι αὐτοι κληρονομησεσι την γην.

Bleſſed are the meek, for they ſhall inherit the earth.

IT appears by no means eaſy to reconcile the promiſe with facts and experience; for earthly proſperity, wealth, power, and pre-eminence, are ſo far from being the inheritance of the meek, that they ſeem to be entirely monopolized by the bold, turbulent, and ambitious; and we may ſay with Cato, This world was made for Cæſar.

To extricate themſelves from this difficulty, ſome commentators have been induced to look out for another earth, which they at laſt fortunately found in the words of St. Peter; who ſays, " Neverthelefs we, ac-" cording to promiſe, look for new heavens " and a new earth, wherein dwelleth righte-" ouſneſs *." To this new earth, they would

* 2 Pet. iii. 13.

perſuade

persuade us, this promise may with propriety be applied, and that therein it will certainly be fulfilled.

But in explaining this passage, there is no occasion to have recourse to so far-fetched and fanciful an interpretation, nor to call in the assistance of a new world. By the meek inheriting the earth, nothing more is meant, than that persons of meek, quiet, and peaceable dispositions, enjoy more happiness on earth, and suffer less disquietude in the present life, than those of opposite characters: and this is verified by the experience of every day; they acquire more friends, and fewer enemies, they meet with fewer injuries and disappointments, and bear those which they cannot avoid with less uneasiness, and pass thro' the world as they do through a crowd, less obstructed, less bruised and jostled, than those, who force their way by violence and impetuosity. To which we may add, that a meek and quiet temper is the most efficacious preservative of health, the first of all earthly blessings, and without which we are incapa-

ble

ble of enjoying any other. Wealth, power, and grandeur, are by no means effential to earthly happinefs; but fhould we admit that they are, and are included in this pro-mife, we fhould not find it altogether unful-filled; for, though the turbulent and over-bearing may fometimes feize on them by violence, they much oftener fail in their at-tempts, and fink by their own infolence into ruin and contempt; whilft thofe of eafy and conciliating manners, filently climb above them, lefs envied, and lefs oppofed, becaufe lefs noticed and lefs offending.

It is univerfally allowed, that nothing fo much advances our worldly interefts, and fo much affifts us in our purfuits of wealth and honours, as good-breeding; and what is good-breeding, but an affectation of meek-nefs, humility, and complacency? if, there-fore, the pretence to thefe amiable qualities can do fo much, furely the poffeffion of them will do a great deal more. In fact it does, and feldom fails to gain us favour, increafe our friends, and advance our interefts.—Thus

we

we fee this promife is generally accomplifhed; the meek do inherit the earth, that is,
have the beft chance of acquiring and enjoying the bleffings of this life, as well as the
happinefs of another.

MATT. V. 7.

Μακαριοι οἱ ἐλεημονες, ὅτι ἀυτοι ἐλεηθη-
σονῖαι.

*Blessed are the merciful, for they shall obtain
mercy.*

CRUELTY is the most unpardonable
of all crimes, because it is without
temptation, and therefore without excuse.
Mercy is the most amiable attribute of God;
and a virtue most becoming the situation of
man, because the sins which he perpetually
commits, and the dangers with which he is
constantly surrounded, oblige him to stand
in need of it every hour : it is peculiarly
congenial to the benevolent spirit of the
Christian religion, and as such is here enforced by the Author of it, in this short but
emphatical declaration ; in which it is remarkable, that we find nothing which limits
our exercise of this amiable virtue within
any bounds, or confines it to any description;

tion; not to our relations, our friends, our neighbours, our countrymen, nor even to mankind: from whence we may reasonably conclude, that he requires us to extend it to every thing that has life and sensibility. The words seem to regard more the disposition of the actor than the object on which it is exerted: " Blessed are the merciful," that is, those who are of a tender and compassionate temper, who feel for the miseries of every thing that has life, and endeavour all in their power to relieve them. Whoever, therefore, can wantonly inflict pain on the meanest animal, or receive a diabolical pleasure from its sufferings, can have no claim to this blessing, nor to obtain that mercy to which he is a stranger.

Matt.

MATT. VI. 16.

Ὅταν δε νηςευητε, μη γινεσθε ὡσπερ οἱ ὑπο-
κριται.

*Moreover, when ye faſt, be not as the hypo-
crites.*

JESUS Chriſt having been born and
educated under the Jewiſh inſtitution,
complied with all the ceremonies and cuſ-
toms of that law, and required none of his
diſciples to relinquiſh them, in order to receive the religion which he came to teach.
Among theſe, faſting at particular ſeaſons
was one, which was commanded by their
law, obſerved by all, and particularly by the
Phariſees, with ſuperſtitious rigour and hypocritical oſtentation; which he here with
ſome aſperity reprehends. He reproves
them, not for faſting, the uſe of which, as
well as that of all the reſt of their religious
rites, he approved and encouraged; but it
is obſervable, that in theſe words there is
nothing

nothing which requires it ; taking it for granted, that they would faſt in obedience to their law, he only ſays, " When ye faſt, be " not as the hypocrites ;" and then proceeds to inſtruct them how to perform this duty in a proper manner : but does not command them to perform it at all.

This ſilence of their maſter, on a ſubject which they thought ſo important, induced many of the Jews, who had become his diſ- ciples, to excuſe themſelves from complying with this unpleaſant ceremony ; as is evident from the queſtion put to him by the diſciples of John the Baptiſt, who ſaid, " Why do we " and the Phariſees faſt often *, but thy diſ- " ciples faſt not ?" From hence it appears plainly, that though Chriſt obſerved this, as well as all the ceremonies of the Moſaic law, it was no part of his inſtitution, nor was en- joined by him as a Chriſtian, or a moral duty. This indeed, and every other mode of ſelf-puniſhment, are ſo oppoſite to the benevolent ſpirit of the religion which he

* Matt. ix. 14.

taught,

taught, that it is impoſſible they can make a part of it. Chriſtianity requires us to make every one as happy as we are able, to relieve the poor, viſit the ſick, and comfort the diſtreſſed; but if every man was obliged to inflict ſufferings upon himſelf, inſtead of excluding miſery at every avenue, as we are benevolently commanded, we ſhould introduce as much as if every man was permitted to injure and torment his neighbour. There are many precepts in the New Teſtament, which require us to ſuffer with fortitude and reſignation, for righteouſneſs ſake, for truth, for our religion, or the benefit of mankind; but we find none which enjoin ſufferings for their own ſake, or repreſent them as meritorious in themſelves. St. Peter exhorts his diſciples to ſuffer patiently for theſe great ends, " becauſe " Chriſt alſo ſuffered for them, leaving us an " example that we ſhould follow his ſteps *;" but he does not adviſe us to ſuffer for no end at all.

* 1 Pet. ii. 21.

Faſting,

Fasting, with all the rest of their religious rites, are continued to the Jews after their conversion to Christianity, but were never imposed on the proselytes of any other nation; from whence it is evident, that Christ never intended by the gospel to abolish the Mosaic law, with regard to the Jews, nor to extend it to any other people. Hence arises that remarkable difference, which cannot escape our notice, between the religion of Christ and that of his Apostles, and particularly of St. Paul; a difference so great, that, if we attend not to the cause of it, we must consider them as two religious institutions contradictory to each other. Christ commands his disciples to perform the most minute ceremonies of the Jewish law, to pay tithes even of mint, anniseed, and cummin *; St. Paul represents the most important, as useless and insignificant, and says, "Circumcision "is nothing, and uncircumcision is nothing, " but the keeping the commandments of " God †." The cause is sufficiently evident:

* Matt. xxiii. 23.   † 1 Cor. vii. 19.

Christ

Chriſt preached to the Jews, and therefore
his religion is founded on and incorporated
with theirs, which he did not require them
to relinquiſh, in order to accept it, and aſſures them, that he did not come " to deſtroy
" their law, but to fulfil it." St. Paul preached chiefly to the Gentiles, but was not com-
miſſioned to convert them to Judaiſm, in
order to their becoming Chriſtians ; and
therefore we do not find that he, or any of
the Apoſtles, impoſed the obſervance of faſts,
or any other ceremonials of the Moſaic law,
on their Gentile proſelytes.

MATT.

MATT. X. 29.

'Ουχι δυο ςρεθια ασσαριε πωλειται, και ἑν εξ αυτων ε πεσειται ἐπι την γην, ανευ τε πα-τρος ὑμων.

Are not two sparrows sold for a farthing?
And one of these shall not fall to the ground
without your heavenly Father.

MANY have been the controversies amongst philosophers, in all times, concerning a general and a particular Providence. Some have been of opinion, that the great Creator of all things so framed the universal system, that every part of it is carried on by a regular process of causes and consequences, without his farther interposition ; and that he cannot interpose, without changing the course of nature by a miraculous act of divine power, which he rarely, if ever, thinks proper to exert: that both the material and moral world are governed by general laws, which cannot be suspended for

the

the fake of individuals, who muft therefore
fubmit to this neceffity, though rewards and
punifhments are not always diftributed in
the prefent life in proportion to their merits;
and that a machine fo conftituted is a more
confpicuous inftance of infinite wifdom and
power, than the one which ftands in need
of the continual interference of its author,
for regulation and fupport.—Others have
thought, that God not only created the
world, but perpetually fuftains, invigorates,
and directs every part of it; and that, if this
energy of divine power was withdrawn but
for a moment, the whole would inftantly
be annihilated.—The latter is undoubtedly
the truth, and is confirmed by reafon, fcripture, and experience. Reafon teaches us
that the revolutions of the vaft and innumerable celeftial orbs, through immenfe fpaces,
or the delicate movements in animal and
vegetable bodies, can never poffibly be performed by any principles originally im-
preffed on matter by attraction, cohefion,
elafticity, or electricity; becaufe they act in
contradiction

contradiction to them all : and therefore they must be effected by the continual direction of some omnipotent hand : it assures us, that the moral, as well as the material world, must be under the continual influence of the same power ; because, without it, the great designs of Providence could never be accomplished. The most important events in life are derived from the operations of matter and will—peace and war, plenty and famine, our health and diseases, our happiness and misery, our safety and destruction. No plan, therefore, could be pursued, if these were all left to the blind movement of the one, or the capricious elections of the other ; but, happily for us, they are both under the controul of an omniscient and omnipotent governor, who dispenses them as seems best to his infinite wisdom ; and this he can do by a perpetual though invisible influence, without the expence of any miracle ; for, if his interference in any event constitutes a miracle, every event is a miracle in nature, because there can be no event without it.

The whole tenour of the scriptures implies

the

the conſtant ſuperintendency of the Creator over all his works, his continual attention to the moſt inconſiderable, as well as to the moſt important events, to the fall of a ſparrow and to the fall of an empire, to ourſelves, our behaviour, our happineſs and ſufferings, our enjoyments, and our wants; theſe are all repreſented as the effects of his will, and therefore the objects of his knowledge and his care; and on this principle we are every where enjoined to love him, to fear him, to praiſe him, to adore him, to obey his commands, to implore his forgiveneſs, to thank him for his mercy, and to deprecate his wrath.

Experience teaches us the ſame leſſon; and a man muſt be poſſeſſed of very little obſervation, and leſs faith, who does not recollect daily inſtances of the apparent interpoſition of Providence in the detection of crimes, the puniſhment of guilt, and the protection of innocence, which fall within the circle of his own knowledge, and are recorded in the moſt authentic hiſtories of all ages.

Matt.

MATT. X. 34, 35.

Μη νομισητε ότι ήλθον βαλειν ειρηνην επι την
γην· εκ ήλθον βαλειν ειρηνην, αλλα μαχαιραν.

Ήλθον γαρ διχασαι ανθρωπον καια τε πα-
ιρος αυτε, και θυγατερα καια της μητρος αυτης, και νυμφην καια της πενθερας αυτης.

*Think not that I am to come to send **peace** on
earth ; I came not to send peace, but a sword.*

*For I am come to set a man at variance
against his father, and the daughter against her
mother, and the daughter-in-law against her
mother-in-law.*

T H I S prophecy of Chrift was foon
compleated and dreadfully fulfilled,
particularly in that city, and amongft that
people to whom it was fpoken; for the
Jews were fo far from accepting that pacific
and benevolent religion which he taught, that
they perverted it into a new caufe of increaf-
ing thofe national contentions and private ani-

mofities in which they were then univerfally involved, and were juftly punifhed for their enormous wickednefs, obftinacy, and incredulity, by the 'fwords of their enemies and their own, with fuch calamities as are unexampled in the hiftory of mankind. This is an undifputed fact; but how is it reconcileable with his frequent declarations on other occafions, and the whole tenour of the New Teftament, in which Chrift every where is ftyled the Prince of peace, and his Gofpel reprefented as introductive of peace and good-will towards men?

The ufual folution of this difficulty is this; That fuch it was intended to be by its benevolent author, but that it was fo far perverted by the wickednefs of man, that the effects of it proved to be the very reverfe of its original defign, and it became productive of all the evils which it was intended to prevent.—But this, I think, is by no means fatisfactory; becaufe I cannot be perfuaded that the wife and beneficent intentions of Providence can ever be defeated by

5   the

the folly and wickedness of man; their effects, indeed, may sometimes be delayed by
events, which to us may seem adverse, but
which, in fact, are necessary to their final
completion; and this, in the present instance,
I take to be the case. The great end of
Christ's coming was to send peace and good-
will amongst men; and this it has undoubtedly effected to a certain degree: his mild
and pacific religion has much abated their
native ferocity, cruelty, and depravity, and
is making a daily progress in this salutary
work; but he found it necessary to send
with it a sword, to lop off some part of that
enormous wickedness, which, at its first appearance, had overspread the world, and to
make men by their sufferings capable of its
reception; as some inveterate diseases will
admit of no remedy without a severe and
painful amputation.

This prophecy of Christ, therefore, is not
in the least contradictory to his own declarations, or the sense of the scriptures, because
they relate to different objects; the first fore-

tells

tells the many miseries which he foresaw men would bring upon themselves, by the abuse and perversion of the religion which he taught them; the latter informs us of the pacific spirit and benevolent design of that religion, and the salutary effects which it must ultimately produce on the morals and happiness of mankind.

M A T T.

Matt. X. 41.

Ὁ δεχομενος προφητην εἰς ὀνομα προφητε μισ-
θον προφητε ληψεῖαι.

He that receiveth a prophet, in the name of a
prophet, ſhall receive a prophet's reward.

BY " a prophet" is here to be underſtood, a
holy, religious, and good man; and the
meaning of the whole ſentence is this : — "He
" that receiveth a prophet," that is, he that
entertains, aſſiſts, and patroniſes a religious
and good man ; " in the name of a prophet,"
that is, becauſe he is, and has the name and
character of a religious and good man ; "ſhall
" receive a prophet's reward ;" that is, is en-
titled to, and ſhall receive as great a reward
as the religious and good man himſelf. That
he ſhould receive an equal reward is perfectly agreeable to divine juſtice, becauſe,
entertaining and patroniſing a pious and virtuous man, from the ſole conſideration of
his merit, demonſtrates a heart as much de-

L 3   voted

voted to piety and virtue as any action which the worthy object of his favour can possibly perform.

If this is true, the converse must be true likewise; that is, that he that entertains, protects, and patronises an impious, a profligate man, for the sake of his vices, is as criminal, and shall receive as severe a punishment, as the most abandoned of his favorites: and this with equal justice, because the approbation of wickedness in others, having no temptation for an excuse, is more atrocious, and demonstrates a more depraved disposition, than even the practice of it. The seduction of pleasure, the lure of interest, or the violence of our passions, may be some, though a poor apology, for the commission of crimes; but to sit cooly by and view with pleasure the iniquities and profligacy of others, and to encourage them by our favour, approbation, and rewards, indicates a disposition more compleatly depraved than the commission of them : but, depraved as it is, we see instances of it every day;

day; we fee the moft impious and profane, the moft corrupt and diffolute, fometimes the idols of the vulgar, and more frequently the idols of the great; we fee them, without any introduction or recommendation, except their vices, entertained, careffed, and patro-nifed by the rich and powerful, who look with envy and admiration on a degree of profligacy in them, which they themfelves are unable to arrive at.

MATT.

MATT. XI. 25.

Ἐν ἐκείνῳ τῷ καιρῷ ἀποκριθεὶς ὁ Ἰησῦς, εἶπεν·
Ἐξομολογῦμαι σοι ϖατερ, κυριε τῦ ῦρανῦ και
τῆς γῆς, ὅτι ἀπεκρυψας ταυτα ἀπο σοφων και
συνετων, και ἀπεκαλυψας ἀυτα νηπιοις.

*Jefus anfwered and faid, I thank thee, O
Father, Lord of heaven and earth, becaufe
thou haft hid thefe things from the wife and
prudent, and haft revealed them unto babes.*

IT feems not a little extraordinary, that
Jefus fhould, in this folemn manner, return thanks to his heavenly Father, for having hid from the wife and prudent the myfteries of that gofpel, which he himfelf came
into the world to promulgate, on the knowledge of which the falvation of mankind depended; but this may be very well accounted for by a proper explanation of thefe
words.

By the " wife," I apprehend, are to be here
underftood, thofe felf-fufficient reafoners

5   who

who will believe no divine revelation which does not exactly tally with their own imperfect ideas of truth, nor obey any precepts which are not conformable to their notions of juſtice and the fitneſs of things. By the " prudent," are meant thoſe, who pay little attention to any religion, but are perpetually employed in worldly occupations, and the purſuits of intereſt and ambition. Jeſus, having experienced the obſtinacy and perverſeneſs, with which perſons under both theſe deſcriptions rejected the revelation which he offered them, and at the ſame time the readineſs with which it was thankfully received by the meek, the humble, the teachable, and the innocent, returns thanks to his heavenly Father, (that is, in the form of an addreſs, adores and admires the wiſdom and juſtice of God), for having ſo contrived the nature of the Goſpel, that it was leſs acceptable, and leſs intelligible to thoſe who, from their evil diſpoſitions, deſerved not to partake of the benefits which it confers, than to thoſe who are more worthy to receive

receive them : and this seems to be nothing more than what we all do, or ought to do, which is, to thank, admire, and adore our gracious Creator, for having so constituted the essence of all human vices and virtues, that each are naturally productive of their own punishments and rewards.

MATT.

MATT. XVI. 18.

Καὶ ἐπὶ ταύτῃ τῇ πέτρα οἰκοδομήσω μɤ τὴν
ἐκκλησίαν.

Upon this rock will I build my church.

FROM this declaration of Chrift it
plainly appears, that he intended to be
the founder of a church, that is, a fociety of
perfons believing his divine miffion, and
openly profeffing the religion which he came
to publifh to mankind; which fociety fhould
be vefted with the powers and privileges of
a corporate body, and exercife them under
his protection to the end of the world; but
we do not find that, by any precepts delivered during his life, or any inftructions left
behind him at his death, he ever communicated to his difciples any plan of the formation of this church, or any rules for the government of it when formed. The reafon of
which I take to be this:—He knew the adminiftration of this government muft fall into

the

the hands of men, be blended with their worldly interefts, and in confequence be foon corrupted and abufed, and therefore unworthy of divine authority ; and that, if he appointed any particular form, or fpecific regulations for the management of it, he muft have given fome degree of fanction to thofe future corruptions and abufes. He knew, likewife, that it was unneceffary ; becaufe a community, once eftablifhed, muft naturally produce rule and fubordination, that is, a government, becaufe it cannot fubfift without one. He inftituted a church, becaufe, without fome inftitution of that kind, his religion muft quickly have been banifhed from the world, and known no where but in the clofets of a few fpeculative philofophers, and therefore had little influence on the general conduct of mankind ; but he chofe rather to truft the form and regulations of it to the nature of man, and the nature of government, than to any pofitive command. He did not ordain that when his religion fhould have fpread over every

quarter

quarter of the globe, this church should become equally extensive, and be governed by one supreme head, his successor and representative. He did not command, that in every respective country this church should be placed under the dominion of bishops or presbyters, of councils, convocations, or synods. He has prescribed no forms of worship, except one short prayer; no particular habits for the ministers who officiate; no places set apart for the performance of religious duties, or decorations for those places to excite reverence and devotion in the performers. All these he has left to the decision of future ages, to be ordered by different communities, in different countries, in a manner that shall best suit the tempers of the people, the genius of their government, and the opinions of the times; provided nothing is introduced inconsistent with the purity of his original institution. From hence evidently appears the ignorance and absurdity of those who reject all ecclesiastical authority as human impositions, and deny the

very

very exiſtence of any Chriſtian church, in contradiction to the expreſs declarations of its founder; and not leſs of thoſe who refuſe compliance with any national religious eſtabliſhment, becauſe they cannot find the form and ceremonies of it exactly delineated and preſcribed in any part of the New Teſtament.

Chriſt has inſtituted eccleſiaſtical, in the ſame manner that God has civil government, that is, by making it neceſſary, without directing the mode of its adminiſtration; becauſe, though the thing itſelf is neceſſary, the mode is not ſo.

MATT.

Matt. XIX. 4, 5.

Ὁ δε ἀποκριθεις, ἐιπεν αὐτοις· Ὀυκ ἀνεγ-
νωῖε, ὁτι ὁ ποιησας ἀπ᾽ αρχης, ἀρσεν και θηλυ
εποιησεν αυτες ;

Και ἐιπεν· Ἑνεκεν τετε καῖαλειψει ἀνθρωπ©.
τον πατερα και την μητερα, και προσκολλη-
θησεῖαι τη γυναικι ἀυτε, και ἐσονται ὁι δυο ἑις
σαρκα μιαν.

*And he answered and said, Have ye not
read, that he which made them at the beginning, made them male and female ;*

*And said, For this cause shall a man leave
father and mother, and shall cleave to his wife:
and they twain shall be one flesh ?*

SHOULD there be any controversy
concerning the lawfulness of polygamy
under the Christian dispensation, this declaration of its author is surely sufficiently de-
cisive in the negative; because, if a man
and a woman, by marriage, become one flesh,
it seems impossible that a greater number

than

than two should be incorporated by that union ; and, if a man is commanded to leave his father and mother, and cleave to one wife, he is surely not at liberty to cleave to another.

The question here put to Jesus was not, indeed, concerning polygamy, but divorce ; but his answer comprehended them both, and declares, by the clearest implication, that the first ought not to be permitted, and, in express words, that the last is absolutely unlawful in all cases, except in that of adultery.

The advocates for polygamy alledge, That the practice of it is recorded as far back as history carries us, to the earliest ages of the world ; that it was allowed during the whole period of the Jewish theocracy, and continued by that people till the coming of Christ, and then not prohibited by any positive command ; and that, therefore, though from a change of circumstances in the present times it may not be expedient, it cannot certainly be unlawful.——This argument has

surely

furely much weight ; but in anfwer it may be faid, That, although we do not find it any where in the New Teftament abfolutely forbid, it is, in this and feveral other places, highly difapproved of by the cleareft implications ; and indeed it is by no means credible, that a cuftom fo licentious, fo injurious to one, and fo deftructive to the domeftic happinefs of both fexes ; a cuftom, even at that time, rejected by almoft all the Gentile nations ; fhould be adopted or permitted under the purity of the Chriftian inftitution.

The true ftate of the cafe I take to be this :—Multitudes of the Jews, unable to refift the preaching of Chrift, and the evidence of his divine miffion enforced by fo many miracles, every day became converts to his religion ; but, being extremely fond of the ceremonies and cuftoms of their own, could not fuddenly be prevailed on to relinquifh them. Of none were they more tenacious than of this of polygamy, in which they and their forefathers had been indulged for fo

many centuries, and which had been authorifed by the example of characters, to whom
they looked up with the moft profound veneration ; and therefore many of them, after
their converfion, continued in the practice
of it.

That they did fo, feems to be confirmed
by what St. Paul writes to Titus, that " a
" bifhop muft be blamelefs, the hufband of
" one wife ;" that is, that although polygamy
might be overlooked in fome of the Jewifh
converts, who could not be prevailed on to
accept Chriftianity on any other terms, it
could not be fuffered in any one who un-
dertook fo important and fo facred an office
as that of a bifhop ; whofe life ought to be
exemplary, and his conduct free even from
the imputation of all blame.—From hence
it appears evident, that polygamy was always confidered, by Chrift and his Apoftles,
as incompatible with the religion which they
taught ; and that, although it might be to-
lerated in fome of the Jewifh profelytes, who
had immemorial cuftom to plead in its be-
half,

half, yet, even in them, it was looked upon as extremely blameable, and was never claimed by or permitted to any of the Gentiles who were converted.

MATT.

MATT. XX. 15, 16.

Ἡ ἐκ ἔξεςι μοι ποιησαι ὁ θελω ἐν τοις ἐμοις; ἡ ὁ ὀφθαλμος σε πονηρος ἐςιν, ὁτι ἐγω ἀγαθος ἐιμι;

Ὁυτως ἐσον]αι ὁι ἐσχατοι, πρωτοι, και ὁι πρωτοι, ἐσχα]οι.

Is it not lawful for me to do what I will with mine own? Is thine eye evil, because I am good?

So the laſt ſhall be firſt, and the firſt laſt.

IN order to underſtand this parable of the houſeholder, who paid his labourers not in proportion to the time in which they worked, or the work which they had per-formed, but according to his own pleaſure; it is neceſſary to remember to whom, and on what occaſion it was ſpoken. Jeſus had juſt before declared, that when he ſhould ſit on his throne of glory, his twelve Apoſtles ſhould ſit on twelve thrones, judging the twelve

twelve tribes of Ifrael. Many of his au-
ditors, who had but lately feen thefe men
employed in the loweft occupations, and by
no means eminent for their virtues or abilities, thought this a very partial declaration,
and this promifed exaltation far fuperior to
their merits. To thefe this parable was
particularly addreffed; intended to teach
them, that all power, glory, and happinefs,
are the fole property of God, and that he
alone has a right to difpofe of them according to his pleafure; that all which we enjoy
is a free gift from his benevolence, and not a
compenfation for our merits; that our merits, if we have any, are derived from him;
that even thefe merits proceed from his
grace, and the rewards of them from his
bounty; that we ought to be thankful for the
benefits we receive from his favor, and have
no pretence to complain of his partiality, if
we fee greater conferred on thofe who may
appear to us to deferve them lefs; that we
are bad judges of the merits of others, and
worfe of our own, and that therefore, in a

M 3   future

future life, many who are now laſt in our eſtimation, will be firſt in happineſs and glory; and many whom we now admire for their virtues, and imagine will be firſt in that ſtate, will be the laſt, that is, leaſt meritorious in the ſight of their juſt and all-diſcerning judge. From whence we may learn, that it is the higheſt preſumption in us to circum-ſcribe the right of our Creator, in the diſtri-bution of his favours, by our imperfect no-tion of fitneſs and equity, to ſet bounds to the operations of any one of his attributes by confronting it with another, to limit his power by the effects of his mercy, or the effects of his mercy by thoſe of his juſtice. His attributes are all above our comprehen-ſion, and therefore we ought only to adore them in ſilence, and ſubmit to his deciſion with gratitude and reſignation.

MATT.

MATT. XXII. 21.

Τοτε λεγει αυτοις· Αποδοʃε εν τα Και-
σαρϴ, Καισαρι· και τα τϗ Θεϗ, τῳ Θεῳ.

*Then said he unto them, Render unto Cæsar
the things which are Cæsar's; and unto God,
the things which are God's.*

IN order to ensnare Jesus into offending
either their own nation, or the Roman
government, under which they were then
subjected, the Jews said unto him, " Tell
" us, therefore, what thinkest thou, Is it law-
" ful to give tribute unto Cæsar, or not ?"
A question the most insidious, and most dangerous to decide on, that art or malice could
have contrived ; because, in the decision of
it, the most important political rights were
to be determined : Whether they, being a
people chosen by God, could lawfully submit to the government of any but God ; or
some one of their own nation, deputed by his

M 4   immediate

immediate direction?—Whether conquest, which is but unjust, though successful violence, can give a just right to govern?—Whether one nation can have a right to rule over, and consequently to impose tribute on another?—And, Whether any sovereign can lawfully compel subjects to pay taxes, without their own consent? If Christ had thought it ever proper for him to give directions on political topics, he certainly would not have neglected this opportunity; but he now, and at all times, industriously avoided it, and said, "Shew "me the tribute money:" then replies to their question, by asking them another, "Whose is this image and superscription?" They answered, "Cæsar's." Then said he unto them, "Render, therefore, unto Cæsar, "the things which are Cæsar's; and unto "God, the things which are God's."

Many opinions, by the ingenuity of commentators, have been extracted from these few words of Christ. Some have thought, that, by them, he intended to explode that

favorite

favorite notion, that they could not be lawfully governed by any except God. Some
have afferted, that, by here acknowledging
the title of Cæfar, he had eftablifhed the
right of all conquerors to rule over the people whom they had fubdued. Others would
perfuade us, that, by the things which are
Cæfar's, are to be underftood, taxes impofed
by the ftate; and, by the things which are
God's, the revenues of the church : and it
is furprifing, that no courtly divine has undertaken to prove, from this fhort decifion,
that every fovereign has a right to feize on
all the money which bears his image and fu-
perfcription. But certainly none of thefe
fanciful conjectures have any foundation in
thefe words of Chrift; which are no more
than an evafive anfwer to an infidious
queftion, and a declaration of what he takes
every opportunity of declaring, That he
did not come to decide political controverfies, to fettle the rights of conquerors
and the conquered, or of fovereigns and fubjects; and that the only inftructions which

he

he could give on that head were, to pay quietly tribute and fubmiffion to whatever government they lived under, without unneceffary inquiries into the lawfulnefs of their claims ; but to inquire diligently after the will of God, and pay the ftricteft obedience to it on every occafion.

M a t t.

MATT. XXVI. 39.

Καὶ προελθὼν μικρον, ἐπεσεν ἐπι προσωπον
αὐτȣ, προσευχομενῳ, καὶ λεʒων, Πατερ μȣ, εἰ
δυνατον ἐʓι, παρελθετω ἀπ᾽ ἐμȣ το ποτηριον
τȣτο.

*And he went a little farther, and fell on his
face, and prayed, saying, O my Father, if it be
possible, let this cup pass from me.*

THE hypothetical words, inserted in
this fervent address of Christ to his
heavenly Father, seem to establish the truth
of two important propositions: First, That
there may be, and actually are, evils inherent
in the nature of things, which even Omnipotence cannot prevent; and, that we have reason to conclude, that all which we suffer in this
life, except such as we bring upon ourselves
by our misconduct or mutual injuries, are of
this kind; that is, such as cannot be prevented without the admission of greater
evils, or the loss of good more than equi-
valent;

valent; becaufe we cannot fuppofe that a Creator of infinite power and goodnefs, would admit any others into any part of his works.

The fecond propofition is, That the fufferings and death of Chrift are likewife of this kind, abfolutely neceffary as an atonement for the fins of mankind, and therefore unpreventable by any power, without defeating the great defign of the benevolent but dreadful tafk which he had undertaken. As fuch they are reprefented, by himfelf and his Apoftles, throughout every part of the New Teftament; not as contingencies, like thofe of other martyrs in the caufe of religion, but as an effential part of the original plan of his miffion. From whence this neceffity arifes, we have not faculties to conceive: but it muft be certainly from fome connections between fuffering and fin, that is, between natural and moral evil, totally beyond the reach of our comprehenfions.

Chrift, under the moft terrible apprehenfions

henſions of his approaching execution, fell on his face, and prayed, ſaying, " O my " Father, if it be poſſible, let this cup paſs " from me ;" that is, if it be poſſible to procure the redemption of mankind without this ſacrifice : but it was not poſſible, and therefore he voluntarily ſubmitted to drink it, as the only means to accompliſh that be-nevolent end ; and, in proof of it, ſays, " No " man taketh my life from me, but I lay " it down of myſelf *." No doubt of its poſſibility could ariſe from any other cauſe, for ſurely it was not only poſſible, but very eaſy, for the power of God to have delivered him out of the hands of man. He might have changed the hearts of his enemies : he might have defeated their malice, by placing him in a ſituation beyond their reach, or by ſending twelve legions of an-gels to his aſſiſtance : " But how then ſhall " the ſcriptures be fulfilled, that thus it muſt " be † ?" that is, How then ſhall the prophe-

* John x. 18.
† Matt. xxvi. 53.

aies

cies and promises be fulfilled, which assure us, that this important purpose can be ef- fected by no other means, nor satisfaction made for the sins of the world on any other terms ?

MARK

MARK II. 27.

Καὶ ἔλεγεν αὐτοῖς· Τὸ σαββαῖον διὰ τὸν ἄν-
θρωπον ἐγένετο, ἐχ ὁ ἄνθρωπ☉ διὰ τὸ σαββαῖον.

*And he said unto them, The sabbath was
made for man, and not man for the sabbath.*

THIS was the reply which Christ
made to the Pharisees, who had frequently reproved him for healing the sick
on the sabbath-day; and, in the present instance, for suffering his disciples to pluck a
few ears of corn as they walked through the
fields on that day; by which we are to understand, that his opinion on this subject was,
that the keeping holy the sabbath-day was a
wise and excellent institution, admirably contrived for the benefit of mankind, but not
of such indispensable importance, that we
should think it is the chief duty of our lives,
or that we were placed in this world on purpose to perform it.

5   The

The Pharifees were a fect of the Jews,
noted for their fpiritual pride and hypocrify,
who pretended to extraordinary fanctity, by
a ftrict and fuperftitious obfervance of every
ceremony appointed by the Mofaic law,
particularly that of keeping holy the fabbath,
with a rigour beyond what the good of fociety would admit, or the inftitution itfelf
required ; and it is not a little remarkable,
that the fectaries of all times have followed
their example in this inftance ; they have
all thought, or pretended to think, that a ri-
gorous obfervance of this day is the firft of
all Chriftian duties, and the neglect of it
the moft enormous of all crimes; whereas,
properly fpeaking, it is no Chriftian duty
at all, in any other fenfe, than that it is the
duty of every Chriftian to comply with every
inftitution, from whatfoever fource it may be
derived, which tends to promote religion
and virtue amongft mankind.

The keeping holy the fabbath-day was
originally enjoined, by a pofitive commandment, to the Jews in the Mofaic law ; and,

as

as fuch, was obferved by Chrift and his
Apoftles, as was every other part of that
law, and was afterwards retained by the
Chriftians of all fucceeding ages, for its peculiar excellence and utility, when all the
reft were laid afide. But I do not recollect
that it is any where injoined by Chrift or
his Apoftles, or even mentioned in the New
Teftament, except in this and fome other
places in which he reproves the Pharifees
for their hypocritical and fuperftitious obfervance of it, by converting a day that was
intended to be fet apart for reft, joy, and
thankfgiving, into a feafon of mortification
and felf-denial of all comforts and conve-
niences of life.

But this leffens not the force of our ob-
ligation to keep this day in a proper manner ; that is, to abftain from labour and all
worldly cares and occupations, and to employ it in acts of devotion, charity, and hofpitality; for which we have the example of
Chrift and his Apoftles, and of every Chriftian church from their times to the prefent

day. The excellence, likewife, of the inftitution itfelf cannot fail to recommend it; for,
certainly, there never was any other fo well
calculated to promote the interefts of piety
and virtue, to call off the worldly-minded
from the perpetual toils of ambition and
avarice, and to give leifure to thofe who are
better difpofed, to improve and cultivate
thofe better difpofitions; to afford relief to
the poor from inceffant labour, and to the
rich from continual diffipation, and to produce fome fenfe of religion in the vulgar,
and fome appearance of it in the great.

MARK

MARK VIII. 38.

Ὃς γαρ ἀν ἐπαισχυνθῃ με και τους ἐμυς λο-
γυς ἐν τῃ γενεᾳ ταυτῃ τῃ μοιχαλιδι και ἁμαρτωλῳ, και ὁ ὑιος τυ ἀνθρωπυ ἐπαισχυνθησεῖαι
ἀυτον ὁταν ἐλθῃ ἐν τῃ δοξῃ τυ ϖαῖρος ἀυτυ, μεῖα
των ἀγῖελων των ἀγιων.

*Whosoever, therefore, shall be ashamed of me,
and of my words, in this adulterous and sinful
generation, of him also shall the Son of man be
ashamed, when he cometh in the glory of his
Father.*

MANY and severe are the threats
which we find denounced by Christ
against hypocrites; that is, against those
who pretended an extraordinary sanctity in
their manners and conversation, without having any true sense of religion or morality in
their hearts. The words before us are a threat,
likewise, against hypocrites, but hypocrites of
a very different sort; those who pretend to
be more profligate than they really are,

N 2 and

and therefore may properly be called hypocrites in wickedneſs. Theſe are much more numerous in the preſent times, and perhaps more miſchievous than the former ; as thoſe do honour to religion and virtue by their pretences to them, theſe affront them by an open diſavowal. Thoſe make others better than themſelves, and theſe worſe, by their example. We meet with this ridiculous and criminal kind of hypocriſy every day ; we ſee men affecting to be guilty of vices for which they have no reliſh, of profligacy for which they have not conſtitutions, and of crimes which they have not courage to perform. They lay claim to the honour of cheating, at the time they are cheated, and endeavour to paſs for knaves, when, in fact, they are but fools. Theſe are the offenders of whom Chriſt will be aſhamed when he cometh in the glory of his Father ; which will be a dreadful but juſt puniſhment, and a proper retaliation of that fooliſh and impious modeſty, which induced them to be aſhamed of him and his word, in complai-
ſance

fance to a finful and adulterous generation;
and to be lefs afraid of incurring the difpleafure of the beft of all Beings, than the
profane ridicule of the worft of men.

Mark

M ARK XVI. 15, 16.

Και ειπεν αυτοις· Πορευθεντες εις τον κοσ-
μον απαντα, κηρυξαλε το ευαγγελιον παση τη
κλισει.

Ὁ πιςευσας και βαπλισθεις σωθησεlαι· ὁ δε
απιςησας, καλακριθησεlαι.

*And he said unto them, Go ye into all the
world, and preach the gospel to every creature.*

*He that believeth, and is baptised, shall
be saved; but he that believeth not, shall be
damned.*

THIS is the commission, together with
the promises and threats annexed to
it, which Christ gave to his Apostles when
he sent them forth to preach the gospel to
every part of the world : in which these three
important questions offer themselves to our
serious consideration; What is meant by believing ? What is meant by being saved ?
and, What by being damned ?—Believing
cannot here be understood to signify the giving

ing affent to the tradition of one church, or
to the creeds and articles of another, or even
to the hiftorical facts recorded in the New
Teftament ; becaufe, at the time when this
commiffion was delivered, no church exifted, no creeds or articles were formed, nor
was the New Teftament written. Believing,
in the language of that book, is for the
moft part ufed as a term fynonymous to that
of becoming a Chriftian. Thus it is related
of the nobleman, whofe fon Jefus had cured,
" Himfelf believed, and his whole houfe *;"
and thus it is faid, that " many of the Jews,
" which had feen the things which Jefus did,
" believed on him †;" that is, were converted
to the religion which he taught, and became
Chriftians ; for which purpofe nothing more
was then required, than to acknowledge that
Jefus was the Son of God (that is, the Meffiah expected by the Jews and foretold by
the prophets), and to receive baptifm as an
external and vifible fign of their initiation

* John iv. 53. † John xi. 45.

N 4 into

into this holy fraternity, which was immediately administered to them on their assenting to this single proposition, as we find it was by Philip to the eunuch, without asking any further questions.

In the next place, What is meant by being saved? In order to understand this expression, it is necessary to recollect that, throughout the New Testament, we are every where informed, that mankind, in the present life, are in a state of guilt and depravity, under sentence of condemnation, and incapable of admission into the kingdom of Heaven; that, in order to redeem them from this unhappy situation, Christ came into the world, and offered them a religion which was effectual for that purpose; and that, whoever shall believe on him (that is, acknowledge his divine authority, accept the religion which he taught, and testify this acceptance by baptism) shall by this, and the atonement made for sin by his sufferings and death, be saved (that is, absolved from their guilt, excused from that sentence, freed from

that

that incapacity, and placed in a state, which, although it may be forfeited by their future misbehaviour, is, in the language of scripture, called salvation). This I take to be the true meaning of being saved; which, without some retrospect, can have no meaning at all.

By being damned, is not here to be understood, being consigned to a state of everlasting punishment, according to the vulgar acceptation of that phrase in our translation, in which sense, I believe, it is no where used by the writers of the New Testament—the original word is καταχριθησεται, *condemnabitur*, which signifies simply, *will be condemned, or found guilty*, without referring to any punishment whatever. In the present instance, it means nothing more than the reverse of being saved. " He that believeth will be saved, but he that believeth not cannot be saved;" that is, Whoever refuses this gracious offer can receive no benefit from it, but must remain in the same state of guilt, condemnation, and exclusion from

the

the kingdom of Heaven, as if no such offer had been made; not as a punishment, but as a neceſſary conſequence of his unbelief. This is not a threat, but a declaration; in which there is no more injuſtice or ſeverity, than in that of a phyſician, who, having preſcribed a ſpecific medicine to a patient labouring under an inveterate diſeaſe, aſſures him, that if he takes it, he will certainly recover; but if he will not, he will as certainly die.——This fair interpretation of this paſſage I think a full vindication of the juſtice and goodneſs of God, from the blaſphemous imputations ſometimes thrown on the divine conduct, in condemning his creatures to eternal miſery, merely for not aſſenting to propoſitions which many cannot believe, and more cannot underſtand; for which there is not the leaſt foundation in the words before us.

LUKE

that incapacity, and placed in a ſtate, which, although it may be forfeited by their future miſbehaviour, is, in the language of ſcripture, called ſalvation). This I take to be the true meaning of being ſaved; which, without ſome retroſpect, can have no meaning at all.

By being damned, is not here to be underſtood, being conſigned to a ſtate of everlaſting puniſhment, according to the vulgar acceptation of that phraſe in our tranſlation, in which ſenſe, I believe, it is no where uſed by the writers of the New Teſtament—the original word is καταχριθησεται, *condemnabitur*, which ſignifies ſimply, *will be condemned, or found guilty*, without referring to any puniſhment whatever. In the preſent inſtance, it means nothing more than the reverſe of being ſaved. " He that believeth will be ſaved, but he that believeth not cannot be ſaved;" that is, Whoever refuſes this gracious offer can receive no benefit from it, but muſt remain in the ſame ſtate of guilt, condemnation, and excluſion from

the

the kingdom of Heaven, as if no such offer had been made; not as a punishment, but as a necessary consequence of his unbelief. This is not a threat, but a declaration; in which there is no more injustice or severity, than in that of a physician, who, having prescribed a specific medicine to a patient labouring under an inveterate disease, assures him, that if he takes it, he will certainly recover; but if he will not, he will as certainly die.—This fair interpretation of this passage I think a full vindication of the justice and goodness of God, from the blasphemous imputations sometimes thrown on the divine conduct, in condemning his creatures to eternal misery, merely for not assenting to propositions which many cannot believe, and more cannot understand; for which there is not the least foundation in the words before us.

Luke

Luke XI. 8.

Λεγω ὑμιν, εἰ και ἐ δωσει αὐτῳ ἀναϛας, δια
ο εἰναι αὐτε φιλον, δια γε την ἀναιδειαν αὐτε
ἐγερθεις δωσει αὐτῳ ὁσων χρηζει.

I say unto you, Though he will not rise and
give him because he is his friend; yet, because
of his importunity, he will rise and give him as
many as he needeth.

THIS parable, and also another of the
importunate widow, in the second chapter, seems to represent the Deity as teazed
into compliance, and granting requests, not
from the reasonableness of the petition, or
the merits of the petitioners, but merely
to put an end to their troublesome im-
portunities. This in man would certainly be a weakness, but in the Supreme
Judge and disposer of all things is an absolute impossibility; and therefore cannot be
the intention of this parable. But, in order
to understand the sense of this, and many
other passages in both the Old and New
Testament,

Teſtament, we ſhould remember, that, although theſe, as well as other writings of remoter ages, abound in more ſublime ideas, and more beautiful figures, than the compoſitions of later ages; yet we muſt not expect to find in them the ſame correctneſs and preciſion. In their ſimiles, provided there were ſome reſemblance in their principal features, little regard was paid to their diſagreement in all the reſt. Thus the pſalmiſt compares the unity of brethren to the precious ointment on the head of Aaron, which ran down to his beard, and even to the ſkirts of his cloathing; between which there is not the leaſt ſimilitude, except that they were both precious and pleaſant things. In their parables and fables, provided the great outlines correſponded with the moral which they deſigned to inculcate, they attended not to the collateral circumſtances which were introduced into the ſtory; and therefore we ought never to draw any concluſions from them. Thus, in the parable of the marriage of the king's ſon, the

king,

king, obferving that one of the guefts had not on a wedding garment, commanded him to be bound hand and foot, and caft into outer darknefs; by which we are taught, that whofoever comes to Chrift, that is, pretends to be a Chriftian, without the proper cloathing of righteoufnefs and faith, will incur his difpleafure, and be feverely punifhed. But we muft not compare the juft difpenfations of Providence, with the unjuft fentence of the king, who punifhed a man for not having on a wedding garment, who had been but juft before picked up in the highway, and could not have been expected to have been properly dreffed for fuch an entertainment.

In like manner, in this parable, the fole intention is to inculcate the duty of fervent and importunate prayer, together with the deferved fuccefs which attends it. This is very well illuftrated by the perfevering importunity of the petitioner, and the compleat though late compliance of his friend. The motive which at laft induced him to comply,

comply, after fo long and obftinate a refufal, is a collateral circumftance, which makes no part of the parable. The parable applies only to the fact, not to the motive which produced it ; and therefore that is not to be attended to.

LUKE

LUKE XI. 24, 25, 26.

Ὅταν το ἀκαθαρτον πνευμα ἐξελθη ἀπο τ8
ἀνθρωπ8, διερχεΙαι δι᾽ ἀνυδρων τοπων ζητ8ν ἀνα-
παυσιν· και μη εὑρισκον, λεγει· Ὑποςρεψω εἰς
τον οἰκον μ8, ὁθεν ἐξηλθον.

Και ἐλθον εὑρισκει σεσαρωμενον και κεκοσ-
μημενον.

Τοτε πορευεται και παραλαμϐανει ἑπΙα
ἑτερα πνευμαΙα πονηροτερα ἑαυτ8, και εἰσελ-
θοντα καΙοικει ἐκει· και γινεΙαι τα ἐσχαΙα τ8
ἀνθρωπ8 ἐκειν8 χειρονα των πρωτων.

*When the unclean spirit is gone out of a man,
he walketh through dry places, seeking rest:
and finding none, he saith, I will return to my
house whence I came out.*

*And when he cometh, he findeth it swept and
garnished.*

*Then goeth he, and taketh to him seven other
spirits more wicked than himself, and they enter
in and dwell there: and the last state of that
man is worse than the first.*

I KNOW of no passage throughout the
New Testament so obscure as this, nor

one

one which the commentators have been so little able to explain :—for which end, it is in the first place necessary to observe, that, in the times in which the gospels were written, an opinion was universally adopted, both by Jews and Gentiles, that madness, idiotism, many of the diseases, and much of the wickedness of mankind, were occasioned by evil spirits, who got possession of their minds and bodies ; and that these spirits, when cast out by some superior power, wandered about in solitary and uninhabited deserts, restless and miserable, until they were able to return to their old, or to occupy some new habitation.

This passage is plainly founded on this idea, and on this supposition will be found not altogether unintelligible ; but may be fairly explained in the following manner :—
" When the unclean spirit goeth out of a man, he, the spirit, walketh in dry places, (that is, wandereth about in dry and sandy deserts) seeking rest ; and finding none, he saith to himself, I will return to my house whence I came out (that is, to the

possession

poffeffion of the fame perfon from whom I have been expelled) and when he cometh there, if he findeth it fwept and garnifhed, (that is, prepared and made ready for his reception by the perfon's relapfe into his former ftate of depravity) then taketh he to him feven fpirits more wicked than himfelf, and they enter and dwell there (that is, they enter and fix their habitation there, and cannot again be caft out) ; fo the laft ftate of that man is worfe than the firft."—The meaning of all which, divefted of metaphor and reduced to common language, I take to be this :—When any one, who has, by the power of reafon and religion, expelled from his heart impious and malevolent difpofi-tions, infufed into it by the operations of evil fpirits, fhall fuffer himfelf again to fall under their dominion, they will return with fevenfold ftrength, and the man will be many degrees more wicked than he was before.

That evil fpirits did, in thofe ages, take poffeffion of the minds and bodies of human beings, we cannot doubt, if we give any credit to hiftory, facred or profane; and, although the fagacity of the prefent more enlightened times hath exploded this opinion with contempt and ridicule, yet we fee daily inftances, which muft induce us to believe, that their power is not even now totally at an end. We fee fome labouring under difeafes which the moft fkilful phyficians are unable to account for or to cure; others perpetrating the moft horrid crimes without provocation, temptation, or advantage: we fee the hand of the fuicide plunging the dagger into his own breaft, in contradiction to his reafon, his principles, and his corporeal feelings: And muft we not conclude, that all thefe unaccountable actions proceed from the directions of fome external powers, which the actors are unable to refift? In madnefs we plainly perceive two diftinct wills operating at the fame time, one of which compels a man to commit the moft outrageous acts, which the other difapproves, but cannot controul; nay, sometimes

ſometimes foreſees, for a conſiderable time, that he ſhall be ſo compelled, but is unable to prevent it.

I cannot conclude this obſervation, without adding another, on the next ſucceeding verſe, in which we are informed, that, " as he " ſpake theſe things, a certain woman of the " company lift up her voice, and ſaid unto " him, Bleſſed is the womb that bare thee, and " the paps which thou haſt ſucked." She had liſtened to his excellent and intelligible diſcourſe for ſome time, which ſhe perfectly underſtood; but when he ſpake theſe things, which were above her comprehenſion, ſhe could no longer forbear lifting up her voice and uttering this pathetic exclamation, to expreſs her applauſe and admiration. This is a picture ſo exactly copied from nature and experience, that we can have no doubt of its truth; and is here only mentioned as a mark of the fidelity with which the moſt minute incidents are recorded by the Evangelical hiſtorians.

LUKE XIV. 10.

'Αλλ' όταν κληθης, πορευθεις αναπεσον εις τον εσχα]ον τοπον.

But when thou art bidden, go and fit down in the lowest room.

CHRISTIANITY is the beft-bred religion in the world, although the manners of fome of its moft rigid profeffors feem to contradict this affertion. There is not a fingle quality required in the compofition of a true Chriftian, which is not equally requifite in the character of a well-bred man ; nor a fingle deviation from politenefs, which does not, under the Chriftian law, become a crime, becaufe it tends to defeat the two great objects of that holy inftitution, which are to promote peace and goodwill on earth, and to qualify us for the kingdom of heaven.

Many were the leffons by which Chrift endeavoured to infufe this amiable virtue

into

into the minds of his diſciples; in the command before us he forbids every inſolent
attempt to precedence, as equally adverſe
to Chriſtianity as to good manners, as it
denotes a proud heart and high ſpirit, inconſiſtent with the humble precepts of that religion. He ſays, " Whoſoever ſhall com-
" pel thee to go a mile, go with him twain,"
that is, In the intercourſes of ſocial life, be
ready to comply with every innocent pro-
poſal, and in every office of civility perform
twice as much, as is either required or expected. This, therefore, is Chriſtianity, as
well as politeneſs.—Again, he ſays, " Whoſo-
" ever ſhall be angry with his brother, with-
" out a cauſe," (that is, ſhall enter into violent, angry, and peeviſh diſputes about nothing) " ſhall be in danger of the judgment
" [or diſpleaſure of God]; but whoſoever
" ſhall ſay to his brother, Thou fool! ſhall
" be in danger of hell-fire;" that is, Who ſhall
make uſe of ſuch opprobrious and affronting
expreſſions as may provoke retaliation and
reſentment, which may end in violence and

O 3   bloodſhed,

bloodſhed, is anſwerable for the conſequences, and therefore ſhall be in danger of
the ſevereſt puniſhment.——Thus we ſee, that
every virtue enjoined by Chriſtianity as a
duty, is recommended by politeneſs as an
accompliſhment. Gentleneſs, humility, de-
ference, affability, and a readineſs to affiſt
and ſerve on all occaſions, are as neceſſary
in the compoſition of a true Chriſtian as in
that of a well-bred man ; paſſion, moroſe-
neſs, peeviſhneſs, and ſupercilious ſelf-ſuffi-
ciency, are equally repugnant to the characters of both :——who differ in this only,
that the true Chriſtian really is what the
well-bred man but pretends to be, and would
be ſtill better bred if he was.

LUKE

LUKE XV. 7.

Λεγω ὑμιν, ὁτι ἑτω χαρα ἑςαι ἑν τῳ
ὑρανῳ ἑπι ἑνι ἁμαρτωλῳ μεϳανοϩντι, ἡ ἑπι ἑν-
νενηκονϳαεννεα δικαιοις, οἱτινες ϩ χρειαν ἑχϩσι
μεϳανοιας.

*I say unto you, That joy shall be in heaven
over one sinner that repenteth, more than over
ninety and nine just persons who need no repentance.*

SOME modern enthusiasts entertain such
favourable ideas of repentance, as to
place it higher, in the catalogue of Christian
virtues, than even perfect innocence itself.
They seem to think, that a man must be a
sinner before he can be a saint; and that, if
his repentance be sincere, his merits will rise
in proportion to his past offences. Nay,
some have gone so far as to recommend
wickedness as preparatory to repentance,
and therefore necessary to insure our salvation. False and impious as these princi-

O 4   ples

ples are, they may, perhaps, like moft errors, have fome foundation in truth mifunderftood; for we certainly fee in this, and many other parts of the New Teftament, an extraordinary degree of merit imputed, and an extraordinary degree of favour fhewn, to earneft and fincere repentance; although repentance, however fincere and fuccefsful, can do no more than place the finner in the fame ftate as if he had never offended. How then comes it to pafs, that we find here a more joyful reception into heaven beftowed upon the finner who hath repented, than upon ninety-nine juft perfons who need no repentance? This feems to be a difpenfation not eafily reconcileable with the wifdom and juftice of God; and therefore I do not apprehend that, by thefe words, any preference is given to finners who repent, above the righteous who need no repentance, becaufe, in fuch a ftate of perfection no human being ever exifted; and therefore the competition can only lie between thofe who have committed great crimes,

of

of which they are truly fenfible, and have fincerely repented, and thofe who have been daily guilty of many fmaller offences, of which they are fo little confcious as to think they need no repentance. This is clearly exemplified by the parable of the Pharifee and the Publican, who went up to the temple to pray*. The Pharifee, unconfcious of his unworthinefs, thought he needed no repentance, and therefore only thanked God that he was not as other men; extortioners, unjuft, adulterous, or even as this Publican : the Publican, fenfible of the many crimes which he had committed, and fincerely forry for them, ftood afar off, and would not fo much as lift up his eyes to heaven, but fmote upon his breaft, faying, " God be merciful to me a finner." " I tell you," fays Chrift, " this man went " down to his houfe juftified rather than the " other."

Perhaps, alfo, there may be fomething in a fincere repentance for paft offences, more acceptable to God, and more congenial to

* Luke xviii. 10.

the

the true spirit of Christianity, and therefore more productive of joy in heaven, than in any degree of original righteousness of which human nature is capable. The painter and the sculptor shew, that beauty cannot be formed by compasses and a rule; a face in which every feature was faultless would be stiff, formal, and unpleasing; there must be some small deviations from exact symmetry, to enable it to strike the eye and captivate the heart of every beholder. Just so in our morals, was it possible for any one to act at all times, and on all occasions, as he ought, his conduct would form a character rather admirable than amiable, unnatural to man, and unlike that of a Christian, because it would certainly be accompanied with some kind of arrogance, self-sufficiency, and independence, inconsistent with the lowliness, humility, and diffidence, essential to that religion. Christianity does not expect that we should be guilty of no offences, but that we be sorry for them. It does not require perfection, of which we are incapable; but a broken

and

and contrite heart, repentance for fins paft, and perpetual endeavours after future a-mendment, which is in every man's power. This is the fole principle on which this holy inftitution is founded, and therefore it is not furprifing that there fhould be extraordinary joy in heaven on every inftance of the falutary effects of it, in the converfion and falvation of a finner.

Experience teaches us, that we receive more joy from the unexpected return of any good, than from the uninterrupted poffeffion of it; from regaining a loft treafure, than from its undifturbed enjoyment; or the recovery of a beloved friend from a dangerous difeafe, than from the knowledge of his continual health. This is both natural and rational, Why then fhould not the angels in heaven be affected with the fame fenfations from the fame caufe?

LUKE

LUKE XVI. 9.

Κᾀγω ὑμιν λεγω· Ποιησαjε ἑαυτοις φιλ8ς ἐκ τ8 μαμωνα της ἀδικιας, ἱνα ὁταν ἐκλιπηjε, δεξωνjαι ὑμας εἰς τας αἰωνι8ς σκηνας.

And I say unto you, Make to yourselves friends of the mammon of unrighteousness ; that, when ye fail, they may receive you into everlasting habitations.

NO commentator, ancient or modern, has yet been able to give us a satisfactory explanation of this exhortation, delivered by Chrift to a very numerous audience: the moft plaufible is this—That by the mammon of unrighteoufnefs, we are to underftand ill-gotten wealth ; and the advice which Chrift here gives to thofe who have fo acquired it, is to employ it in acts of charity and beneficence, by which means, though they fail in other parts of their duty, they may obtain admiffion into everlafting life.—This interpretation might do very well,

if

if the words would bear it; but it is certainly impoffible, by any torture, to extract out of them such a meaning; and if such a meaning could be allowed, it would not in the leaft correfpond with the preceding parable: in order to underftand which, as well as the words before us, it is neceffary to recollect, both on what occafion they were fpoken, and to whom they were addreffed.

We find, in the foregoing chapter, that whilft Jefus was delivering thefe feveral parables to a very great multitude, he obferved amongft them fome Pharifees attending in the crowd; a fet of men who were perpetually employed in external acts of piety and devotion, and as conftantly bufied in every fpecies of extortion and fraud. To thefe Pharifees, equally remarkable for their religion and their roguery, this exhortation was with peculiar propriety addreffed; in which, I apprehend, we are to underftand, by the mammon of unrighteoufnefs, the kingdom of Satan; the exiftence of which was univerfally believed in thofe

times,

times, and is frequently mentioned or al-
luded to in the scriptures, and placed in op-
position to the kingdom of God. The advice here given to these men is this—not
to attempt, at the same time, to serve God
and Mammon; but, when they, by their
iniquities, have lost all hopes of admission
into the kingdom of light, to secure a
reception in the kingdom of darkness,
and to imitate the example of the unjust
steward, in the parable which he had just
before delivered to them, who, having abandoned all expectations of future support
from his lord, on account of his misbehaviour, and endeavoured to conciliate to himself the goodness of his tenants, that when
he was put out of the stewardship, they
might receive him into their houses; for
which artful precaution his lord commended
him, because he had done wisely, but totally
rejected him because he had not done ho-
nestly.—This, I think, is a just and fair explanation of this abstruse passage; which
seems to be rather an ironical reproof of the

5   Pharisees

Pharisees for their hypocrisy and avarice, than a serious direction for their conduct, and bears some resemblance to what Joshua said to the Israelites; " If it seem evil unto " you to serve the Lord, choose you this day " whom you will serve *:" so Christ says, If you will not be subjects of the kingdom of God, make yourselves friends in the kingdom of Satan.

---

* Joshua xxiv. 15.

LUKE

LUKE XVI. 25.

Εἶπε δὲ Ἀβρααμ· Τεκνον, μνησθηῆι ὁτι
ἀπελαβες ου τα ἀγαθα σ8 ἐν τῇ ζωῇ σ8, και
Λαζαρος ὁμοιως τα κακα· νυν δὲ ὁδὲ ϖαρακα-
λεῖαι, συ δὲ ὀδυνασαι.

*But Abraham faid, Son, remember that thou
in thy life-time receivedft thy good things, and
likewife Lazarus evil things: but now he is
comforted, and thou art tormented.*

ALL the commentators on this parable
feem to have miftaken the intention
and moral of it; they have all underftood it,
as defigned only to inform us, that no judgment can be formed of men's condition in a
future life, by the appearances in the prefent,
of either their profperity or diftrefs: that the
rich and great will, if criminal, certainly meet
with the punifhment due to their offences, in
another ftate, which, by the influence of their
power, they may have evaded in this; and the
poor and difeafed, if virtuous, will there receive

ceive retribution for all the miseries and ill-treatment which they have undeservedly suffered. In order to accommodate the parable to this interpretation, they have constantly painted the character of Dives in the blackest, and that of Lazarus in the brightest colours; for which there is not the least foundation in the parable itself, as there is not one word said of the criminality of the one, or the merits of the other; Abraham, in his answer to the rich man, does not bid him to remember, that he acquired his wealth by fraud or rapine, or that he had expended it in profligacy or oppression; and that, therefore, he ought not to complain of a punishment which he had so justly deserved. He says nothing of the virtues of Lazarus, that he had been pious, sober, honest, and patient; he only answers the complainant in a friendly manner, " Son, remember that thou in thy " life-time receivedst good things, and like- " wise Lazarus evil things; but now he is " comforted, and thou art tormented :" by which, I apprehend, he means to address

Vol. IV.   P   him :—

him:—"Son, although thy prefent fituation
is very wretched, and that of Lazarus no lefs
happy, thou haft no reafon to arraign the
partiality of God; but oughteft to remember,
that thou, in a former ftate, enjoyedft all the
pleafures of wealth and profperity, and that
then Lazarus fuffered all the miferies of poverty and difeafe, but that now he is comforted, and thou art tormented, in conformity to
that impartial and eternal law of Providence,
which inftituted the perpetual rotation of
good and evil."

From this parable we may learn, that
the Supreme difpofer of all things diftributes
good and evil amongft his creatures, not
only with juftice, but with a greater degree
of equality than we imagine; and that this
he is enabled to perform by having fo won-
derfully contrived the difpofition of things,
and the conftitution of man, that riches,
power, wealth, and profperity, in this life,
actually lead him into many vices, which
will incur punifhment in another; and fick-
nefs, poverty, and diftrefs, are as naturally
productive

productive of many virtues, which will there merit a reward ; by which means happinefs and mifery are more equally diftributed, at the fame time that ftrict juftice is done to every individual according to his deferts, and no one can have any caufe to complain.

This idea of the rotation of good and evil, of enjoyments and fufferings, is confirmed by the cleareft allufions in feveral parts of the New Teftament; for inftance, we there read, that " it is eafier for a ca- " mel to go through the eye of a needle, " than for a rich man to enter into the " kingdom of God *;" not becaufe it is criminal to be rich, but becaufe, whilft riches beftow on their poffeffors many prefent gratifications, they ufually make them proud, infolent, and profligate, which incapacitates them from becoming members of that holy and happy community. Again, it is faid, " Bleffed are thofe that mourn, for they " fhall be comforted †;" not becaufe there is any merit in mourning, but becaufe

* Matt. xix. 24.   † Matt. v. 4.

afflictions

afflictions naturally tend to make men humble, sober, patient, and virtuous in this life, for which they will deserve and receive a recompence of comfort in another. This wise disposition of Providence, in the general course of things, although it marks his impartiality, is no impediment to his justice, because it lays no one under compulsion, and may be interrupted by the conduct of every individual. The rich are not obliged to be wicked, nor the poor to be virtuous; a rich man may employ his wealth in such a manner in this life, as to acquire happiness by it in another; and a poor man may be so incorrigible as to make himself very miserable in both. All that we are to learn from it is, to take extraordinary care to avoid those crimes to which our situation renders us peculiarly liable.

J O H N

JOHN III. 3.

Ἀπεκριθη ὁ Ἰησες, και ειπεν αὐτω· Ἀμην ἀμην λεγω σοι, ἐαν μη τις γεννηθη ἀνωθεν, ἐ δυναlαι ἰδειν την βασιλειαν τε Θεε.

Jesus answered, and said unto him, Verily, verily, I say unto thee, Except a man be born again, he cannot see the kingdom of God.

THE meaning of which is this :—That mankind are born or come into the world with difpofitions fo depraved, fo prone to anger, malice, revenge, avarice, and am-bition, that it is impoffible for them ever to enter into the kingdom of Heaven, except they are fo totally changed as to become new creatures. No partial alteration will do ; it muft be an entire change of temper, fentiments, habits, manners, inclinations, and purfuits. All thefe turbulent and high-fpi-rited paffions muft be eradicated, and meek-nefs, gentlenefs, and poornefs of fpirit, in-

P 3   troduced

troduced in their room; anger muſt give place to patience, malice to benevolence, revenge to forgiveneſs, and all worldly purſuits to a conſtant habit of piety and devotion. This, in the language of ſcripture, is properly and emphatically ſtyled being born again; becauſe it is a kind of entrance upon a new life, and a commencement of a ſtate entirely different from the former. The neceſſity for this change is ſufficiently evident, becauſe, if men could be permitted to carry theſe evil diſpoſitions with them into the kingdom of God, they would not be happy themſelves, nor ſuffer others to be ſo.

We ſee that even upon earth, if a wicked, malignant, and turbulent man was confined for life, in a virtuous, peaceable, and pious ſociety, it would be no inconſiderable puniſhment; and much more ſevere would it be in heaven, where the contraſt is greater and the duration longer. Wickedneſs and miſery are by nature ſo cloſely united, that they cannot be ſeparated, and therefore neither

ther of them can have a place in the kingdom of God. If any one's difpofitions are
cruel, malignant, envious, turbulent, factious, and ambitious, though, in contradiction to their impulfe, he fhould perform all
the duties of piety, benevolence, humility,
and fubmiffion, he could not become a
member of this holy and happy fociety, becaufe his admiffion would be rather a punifhment than a reward: before he could
attain this ftate of felicity, he muft be qualified to enjoy it, and this can only be effected by being born again. How a man
is to be born again, Jefus further informs
us in the fucceeding verfe; he there fays,
" Except a man be born of water and of
" the Spirit, he cannot enter into the king-
" dom of God;" that is, except a man be
born again, by embracing the doctrines and
obeying the precepts of his religion, for
which purpofe the external fign of baptifm,
and the internal affiftance of the Holy Spirit,
are abfolutely neceffary. By thefe, together
with fincere repentance and reformation, he

P 4   may

may become a new perfon, and perfectly qualified to be, and to make others happy in that bleffed community; and when qualified, however great may have been his former offences, he will be readily admitted, and there will be joy in heaven at his reception.

John

JOHN VI. 44.

Οὐδεις δυναῖαι ἐλθειν προς με, ἐαν μη ὁ πατηρ
ὁ πεμψας με, ἑλκυση αὐτον.

No man can come to me, except the Father,
which hath sent me, draw him.

MOST of our commentators, appre-
hensive lest the obvious sense of
these words would lead them into difficulties concerning the grace of God, and the
free-will of man, which they were unable
to solve, have endeavoured to explain them
away, and substitute other significations, for
which there is no authority. The true meaning I take to be this :—" No man," says
Christ, " can believe the doctrines, or obey
the precepts, which I teach, except he is enabled by the assistance and grace of God :" by
which we are not to understand any sudden
irresistible impulse, as some enthusiasts would
persuade us; but, except God shall be
pleased to dispose his heart, and also the

circumstances

circumſtances of his ſituation, in ſuch a manner as to draw him into the right road of
faith and obedience. This is the declaration of Chriſt, and the doctrine univerſally
enforced by all the writers of the New Teſtament. St. Paul ſays, " Not that we are ſuf-
" ficient of ourſelves to think any thing as of
" ourſelves, but our ſufficiency is of God *."
He ſays alſo to the Philipians, " For it
" is God which worketh in you both to will
" and to do, of his good pleaſure †". This
is the conſtant language of the ſcriptures;
in which we are every where exhorted to
ſeek, to depend on, to hope for, and to pray
for this divine influence on our thoughts
and actions, as neceſſary to our thinking any
thing right, or performing any thing good :
and yet we are conſtantly conſidered, by
the whole tenour of thoſe writings, as free
agents, poſſeſſed of perfect liberty to do
good or evil, and as ſuch we are inſtructed,
admoniſhed, tempted by rewards, and threat-
ened with puniſhments. How contradic-

* 2 Cor. iii. 5. † Phil. ii. 13.

tory

tory foever thefe two propofitions may feem, they are both undoubtedly true. Of the firft we cannot fail of being convinced by reafon, nor of the latter by experience. Reafon affures us, that no creature can think or act independant of his Creator, in whom he lives, and moves, and has his being, and from whom he receives power to think or act at all; and it feems indeed impoffible that a Creator, however omnipotent, fhould beftow on his creatures fuch a degree of freedom as to make them independent of himfelf: for he muft infufe into their original frames fome difpofitions, good or bad; he muft give them reafon fuperior to their paffions, or paffions uncontrouled by their reafon; he muft endue them with a greater or lefs degree of wifdom or folly; he muft place them within or beyond the reach of temptations, and within the view of virtuous or vicious examples. All thefe circumftances muft proceed from his difpenfations, and from thefe their elections

and

moral inftitution which ever ventured to affert the truth of them both; which, as they are both undoubtedly true, feems no inconfiderable proof of the fupernatural information and authority of that difpenfa-tion.

than being intimately united to him, by believing his doctrines and obeying his precepts; and that, when applied to the bread and wine received in the facrament, they mean only that thefe are fymbols of his fufferings and death. But they are furely too expreffive, too much infifted on, and too often repeated, to admit of fo cold an interpretation; nor is it credible that Chrift would have made ufe of an expreffion for the fake of metaphor, which fhocked his hearers, offended his difciples, and has produced the moft violent contentions amongft them from that time to the prefent hour.

The Evangelifts who heard them, and have fo emphatically recorded them, had very different ideas of the importance of thefe words, and fo had St. Paul, who reproved the Corinthians who received unworthily, by not difcerning the Lord's body; that is, by not perceiving that they were then not eating and drinking bread and wine as their daily food, but fomething which, by powers fupernaturally annexed to

5   it,

it, would produce the moſt important effects on their preſent diſpoſitions and future happineſs. Our firſt reformers, though
they rejected tranſubſtantiation, yet retained
the higheſt veneration for this ſacrament,
the ſanctity of the elements, and the importance of their effects on the communi-
cants ; and I am inclined to think, that they
underſtood the ſenſe of the ſcriptures better,
and the true ſpirit of Chriſtianity more cor-
rectly, than our preſent reformers of reformation. Theſe ſet up reaſon as the meaſure of truth, and then pare away the ſcriptures to make them fit it : thoſe ſearched
them with diligence and candour, to find
out their true and genuine ſignifications,
without any regard to the deciſions of human reaſon ; from hence they formed their
opinions and doctrines, and from them their
creeds and articles; and on this principle we
ought to ſubſcribe them—by which we do
not aſſert their truth, but their conformity
to the ſenſe of the ſcriptures, which they
were intended to explain : the truth and
authority

authority of thofe writings is another queſtion.

Several of our modern divines repreſent
the ſacrament of the Lord's ſupper as a
mere commemoration of his ſufferings and
death; by which they entirely deſtroy the
end and intent of it: for, although this is a
poſitive inſtitution, it is of a moral nature,
becauſe it is deſigned to drive the wicked
into repentance and amendment; and for
this purpoſe it is moſt admirably contrived,
becauſe, if they have not totally rejected the
Chriſtian ſcheme, it lays them under inſu-
perable difficulties, as it obliges them either
to augment their guilt, by the neglect of a
poſitive command, or, by obeying it without repentance and reformation, to ratify
their own condemnation. But if theſe very
extraordinary words of Chriſt have no meaning, or mean nothing more than a bare
commemoration—if conſecration confers no
ſanctity on the bread and wine—if thoſe who
receive them worthily receive no benefit,
nor thoſe who receive them unworthily in-

cur no danger—the inftitution is vain and ufelefs, and has no more concern with our religion or morals than the commemoration of gunpowder treafon, or of any other event recorded in the hiftory of former times.—Although, therefore, we cannot believe, in contradiction to our fenfes, that by thefe emphatical words of Chrift the material fubftance of the elements is changed; yet, furely, we may believe, without the imputation of credulity, that they have fome meaning; and that, by them, powers, property, and effects may be annexed to the proper ufe of the facrament, which may greatly contribute to our obtaining pardon for our paft offences, prevent us from falling into future tranfgreffions, and effentially affift us in our progrefs to everlafting life.

JOHN

JOHN VII. 46.

Οὐδέποτε ὕτως ἐλαλησεν ἀνθρωπΘ‑, ὡς οὗτΘ‑ ὁ ἀνθρωπΘ‑.

Never man fpake like this man.

I HAVE always been of opinion, that the moſt convincing proof of the divine authority of the Chriſtian revelation may be drawn from the originality of its doctrines, precepts, and the character of its author. This religion teaches us, that mankind come into the world in a ſtate of depravity, guilt, and condemnation, from which they cannot be redeemed, but by the merits and mediation of Jeſus Chriſt, together with their own ſincere repentance, reformation, and faith in him; and that, on theſe terms, God will accept his ſufferings and death, as an atonement for their ſins; but that theſe terms they are unable to comply with, without the ſuperintendency of his grace and aſſiſtance, although they are endued with

Q 2   perfect

perfect free-will, and are accountable for the use of it.—All these doctrines are so entirely new, that they had never entered into the head of any one before, and never any man, but this man, had thought or spake any thing like them. Imposture always puts on the garb of truth, and resembles her as near as she can; but in all these propositions there appears not even a pretence to probability, and therefore, as they cannot be invention, we may reasonably conclude that they must be true.

The moral precepts of this institution are, indeed, similar to those of all others; but in this respect they also are entirely new, that they are carried to a higher degree of purity and perfection, than was ever thought of by the legislators and philosophers of preceding ages. They had some distant prospect of a future state of rewards and punishments, but they saw it through a glass darkly, obscured by clouds of doubt and uncertainty; but this man spake of it with

certainty

certainty and authority, removed all the in-
tervening clouds, and shewed it in the cleareft
day-light.

The character of the great author of this
difpenfation, is not lefs new than the religion itfelf; there is no inftance, in the hiftory of mankind, of the founder of a religion,
who propofed by it no benefit to himfelf,
as well as to the world, who intended not
to acquire wealth, power, and dominion
over his followers; nor an inftitution in the
conftruction of which this intention is not
evidently vifible. But Chrift difavows all
pretences to fuch acquifitions, chofe nothing
for himfelf, and promifed nothing to his
difciples but poverty, difgrace, fufferings,
and death.

The progrefs of this religion was equally
new and unprecedented with all the reft;
for in the courfe of a few years it triumphed
over all oppofition, from reafon and philofophy, from principalities and powers, and
fpread itfelf over all the moft civilized
and learned countries then in the world.

This

This verified the wife prediction of Gama-
liel; who faid to the High-prieft, defirous of
perfecuting the Apoftles, " Let them alone ;
" for if this counfel or work be of men, it
" will come to nought ; but if it be of God,
" ye cannot overthrow it *."

         * Acts v. 38, 39.

JOHN

JOHN XVIII. 40.

'Εκραυγασαν ꭒν παλιν παντες, λεγοντες·
Μη τꭒτον, αλλα τον Βαραββαν· ην δε ὁ Βα-
ραββας λῃςης.

*Then cried they all again, saying, Not this
man, but Barabbas. Now Barabbas was a
robber.*

IT has frequently been well obferved, that
the Supreme difpofer of all things never
interpofes a fupernatural power, whenever
his defigns can be accomplifhed by ordinary
means; that is, by the paffions and actions
of free beings; the effects of which are as
certain and uniform, as thofe of matter and
motion; and which, though to us not fo
vifible, are as accurately known by him,
who is perfectly acquainted with their frames
and difpofitions, from whence their actions
muft inevitably be derived.

This is remarkably exemplified in the
Evangelical hiftory of the life and death
of

of Jefus Chrift; in which we fee that, in order to afcertain his divine miffion, and give
a fanctity to the religion which he taught,
miraculous works were every day performed,
becaufe this could not have been effected
without them; but the whole progrefs of
his perfecutions, fufferings, and death, were
left to the ordinary operations of the malevolence, wickednefs, and ignorance of mankind, the ufual inftruments which Providence employed to bring about the moft
important events: and by thefe we find that
this, the moft important of all others, was
effected, without the affiftance of any fupernatural power; for no fooner did Jefus
enter upon his benevolent office of inftruct-
ing and reforming mankind, than he was
mifunderftood by fome, and mifreprefented
by others; he was reviled, infulted, and
perfecuted, his doctrines were called blaf-
phemy, and his miracles imputed to the
devil. In a little time the Jewifh prieft-
hood (apprehenfive from his preaching of
danger to their church) and the civil ma-
giftrates

giftrates (fearful of infurrection in the ftate)
united to deftroy him. Falfe witnefses were
fuborned to accufe him, and one of his own
difciples was corrupted to betray him. He
was then brought before the judgment-feat
of a Roman governor, who, though he declared that he found no fault in him, yet
(fearing to offend the moft powerful part
of the nation over which he prefided, and
ftill more overawed by the name of Cæfar)
preferred his own intereft to the protection
of friendlefs innocence, and condemned him
to a cruel and ignominious death. But it being cuftomary, at this time of the paffover,
to releafe one malefactor at the requifition of
the people, and there being now one under
fentence of condemnation, called Barabbas,
this timid judge propofed an option to the
populace, which of them he fhould releafe,
hoping that they would do that juftice
which he himfelf had not courage to perform. But here a meek and virtuous character had no chance, in a competition for
popularity with one who, though a robber,
had

had been the ringleader of an insurrection; and therefore they all cried out, again and again, "Not this man, but Barabbas." All this was but the ordinary process of human wickedness, ignorance, and malevolence; and no miraculous interference appears in any part of this transaction, because none was wanted. For, certainly, no miracle is requisite to produce opposers of truth, enemies to reformation, persecutors of innocence, and magistracy tenacious of their authority ; a priesthood jealous of their power, a servant bribed to betray his master, false witnesses, a self-interested judge, and a profligate and misled populace. These are the growth of every age and country in the world, and were fully sufficient to accomplish this important and astonishing event; and will ever remain a remarkable instance, that the worst actions of the worst of men are sometimes made use of, by the power and wisdom of God, to carry into execution his most beneficent and salutary designs.

JOHN

John XX. 29.

Λεγει αυτω ὁ Ἰησες· Ὁτι ἑωρακας με,
Θωμα, πεπιςευκας· μακαριοι οἱ μη ἰδοντες,
και πιςευσαντες.

*Jesus saith unto him, Thomas, because thou
hast seen me, thou hast believed : blessed are they
that have not seen, and yet have believed.*

WHAT! says the self-sufficient rea-
soner, are those the most blessed
who believe without proof? And is the merit of faith greater, in proportion as the evidence for it is less?—To such querists I
shall only answer, That they understand not
the nature of faith, nor in what the merit of
it consists.   In the mere assent to a proposition, there is no merit; because, if the
proof is obscure, it is weakness; if clear, it
is compulsion.   It is not the *act*, but the
disposition, which places faith so high in
the catalogue of Christian virtues, and renders infidelity so criminal.   One of the chief
characteristics

characteristics of Christian charity is, that it believeth all things; because this readiness to believe must proceed from an humble, submissive, and teachable temper. Whereas incredulity, when the evidence is sufficient, generally arises from men's vices, and at best, from a self-conceited, suspicious, and untractable disposition, which is utterly incompatible with the whole tenour of that religion. This seems to have been the case of St. Thomas; who is here reproved for not believing the resurrection of Christ, on the positive and unanimous testimony of all the Apostles (with whose honesty and veracity he was perfectly acquainted, and had no reason to question) because he had not seen him with his own eyes, and felt him with his own hands : and, perhaps, he was not indulged with so incontestible proof as the rest had been, in order to try and correct this incredulous and suspicious disposition. If this was really the fact, we may from thence reasonably conclude, that many things are communicated to us, in the scrip-

tures,

tures, in a manner not so perfectly clear and demonstrative as they might have been, for the same cause, that is, to try and cultivate in us a disposition so necessary in the composition of a Christian.

ROMANS VIII. 29.

Ὅτι ὃς προεγνω, και προωρισε συμμορφὲς της
εἰκονος τὲ ὑιὲ αὑτὲ.

For whom he did foreknow, he also did pre-
deſtinate.

MUCH unneceſſary labour has been
employed, by many learned divines
and metaphyſicians, to reconcile the foreknowledge of God and the free-will of
man; which never can be at variance, becauſe they have nothing to do with each
other. The Apoſtle here ſays, " Whom he
" did foreknow, he alſo did predeſtinate;"
that is, Thoſe whom he foreknew would be
wicked, he foreknows will be puniſhed; and
thoſe whom he foreſees will be righteous, he
foreſees alſo will be rewarded: but they are
not wicked and puniſhed, or righteous and
rewarded, becauſe he foreknows it; but he
foreknows it becauſe they are ſo. It is
impoſſible but that an omniſcient Being,

5   " in

" in whom we live, and move, and have " our being," muſt foreſee all our thoughts and actions, and the conſequences which attend them, and therefore muſt foreknow our deſtination in the preſent, and in a future life: but his foreknowledge is not the cauſe of it, nor in the leaſt controuls the freedom of our elections, in which we enjoy as perfect liberty as if they were totally unknown; for the mere knowledge of one being, cannot poſſibly have any influence on the actions of another. If any man is well acquainted with the diſpoſitions of another, he may nearly gueſs how he will conduct himſelf on any occaſion; if he knows they are profligate and prodigal, he may reaſonably conclude that he will deſtroy his health, waſte his fortune, and die in an hoſpital or a gaol; this accordingly happens, but not becauſe he had foreſeen it; that could not be the cauſe of this man's miſbehaviour or misfortune; which could be derived only from his own folly and extravagance. What is but conjecture in man, in God is certain prefcience; but the elections of free agents are no more controuled by the one than the other.——In this, I perceive nothing abftrufe, difficult, or in the leaft inconfiftent with the juftice of God, or the free-will of man. The caufe of all our embarraffments on this fubject I take to be this :——From the nature of human conceptions and human language, we are under the neceffity of applying ideas and expreffions, relative to time, to the exiftence, the attributes, and actions of the Supreme Being; with which they have no kind of relation; which leads us into innumerable abfurdities in our fpeculations on this fubject. With God there is no paft, prefent, and to come: he knows all things equally at all times, and therefore cannot properly be faid to foreknow or predeftinate any thing. This foreknowledge may be to him predeftination; but with regard to us, as it affects not our conduct, it is in a moral fenfe abfolutely nothing.

ROMANS

ROMANS XIII. 1, 2.

Πασα ψυχη ἐξεσιαις ὑπερεχεσαις ὑποτασ
σεσθω. Οὐ γαρ ἐςιν ἐξεσια εἰ μη ἀπο Θεε· αἱ
δε ἐσαι ἐξεσιαι, ὑπο τε Θεε τεταγμεναι
εἰσιν.

Ὡςε ὁ ἀντιτασσομενος τη ἐξεσια, τη τε
Θεε διαταγη ἀνθεςηκεν· οἱ δε ἀνθεςηκοτες,
ἑαυτοις κριμα ληψονται.

*Let every soul be subject unto the higher powers: for there is no power but of God; the
powers that be are ordained of God.*

*Whosoever, therefore, resisteth the power,
resisteth the ordinance of God: and they that
resist shall receive to themselves damnation.*

THROUGHOUT the whole New
Testament we find, that both Christ
and his Apostles were particularly careful
to avoid giving any instructions concerning
government, and on all subjects of a political nature; an example which the preachers of his gospel would do well to imitate

in

in all times. The paſſage here before us is almoſt the only deviation from this general rule, and is a ſtrong inſtance of the wiſdom and neceſſity of this extraordinary caution; for, although it is nothing more than a general exhortation to obedience, it has at all times been perverted to ſpeak the language, and ſerve the iniquitous purpoſes, of contending parties. The advocates for arbitrary power, and flatterers of princes, have endeavoured to prove from it, that all ſovereigns are veſted, by divine appointment, with uncontroulable authority, accountable for the uſe of it to God alone, from whom they receive it; which no ſubject, however oppreſſed, can reſiſt, without reſiſting the ordinance of God, and incurring a puniſhment due to ſo preſumptuous a crime. —On the other ſide, the friends of liberty, who are enemies to all power in any hands but their own, connect theſe words with thoſe in the ſucceeding verſe, which declare, that " rulers are not a terror " to good works, but to the evil;" and from

thence

thence would perfuade us, that whenever a government is fo much perverted from its original defign, as to become a terror to good works, and not to evil (that is, whenever it is unjuftly and tyrannically adminifter-ed) it becomes then not only our right, but our duty, to refift it. But in this, as in moft controverfies, both fides are in the wrong; for, if the arguments of the former were univerfally to prevail, there could be no liberty, if of the latter, no government, upon earth; but certainly Chriftianity never intended to make men either flaves or re-bels. We have here a wife and falutary in-junction from St. Paul, to his difciples then at Rome, to fubmit quietly to any govern-ment under which they lived, without mak-ing any nice inquiry into the rights of thofe who govern, or factious objections to their adminiftration; which is not in the leaft difpenfed with by the following words; that " rulers are not a terror to good " works, but to evil;" which are added as a farther argument to induce all good men to

fubmit

submit to and support government, because it is instituted for their protection; and we cannot suppose that the Apostle could mean by them to furnish the Christians with an excuse for disobedience, as his whole intention is clearly to enjoin them to submit peaceably to the Roman government, which was then, in the truest sense, a terror to good works, and not to evil; and particularly to their good works, for which they were daily oppressed and persecuted. The doctrine of St. Paul is plainly this, That every man ought to be subject to the powers that be (that is, to the established government of the country in which he lives) for this wise and pious reason, because all power must be derived from the appointment, or at least from the permission, of God; and this not only for wrath, but for conscience sake, (that is, not only for fear of incurring the displeasure of that government, but as a duty required by him). This also is the doctrine of Christ himself, which he enforced, both by his precepts and example, on all

5   occasions.

occasions. When Pilate said unto him,
" Knowest thou not that I have power to
" crucify thee, and have power to releafe
" thee?" he anfwered, " Thou couldft have
" no power againft me, except it was
" given thee from above;" and therefore he
fubmitted.

There may be cafes in which refiftance of
the fupreme power may be juftified by neceffity, but fuch ought never to be defined
or pointed out before their arrival; when
they come, they will fpeak for themfelves,
and men will be ready enough to hear
them. Refiftance may fometimes be practifed, but ought never to be preached, for
we ftand in need of no leffons to teach us
difobedience; and therefore we do not find,
throughout the whole New Teftament, one
definition or recommendation of civil liberty, nor one command to fight or die in
its defence. Thefe may be the glorious at-
chievements of heroes and patriots; but thefe
are not lifted under the banners of Chrift;
the glory, as well as the duty, of his difci-

ples

ples are, to fuffer and fubmit.—We fhould
remember alfo, that by refiftance, not only
force and open rebellion is here to be underftood, but all fecret machinations, and all
turbulent and factious endeavours to diftrefs
and impede government, arifing from motives of felf-intereft, ambition, or difappointment. Thefe are, in fact, rebellion, with
this only difference, that they are more
treacherous and cowardly, more likely to
fucceed, and lefs to be punifhed, and are
therefore equally forbid under the denunci-
ation of the fame tremendous penalty.

1 CORIN-

1 CORINTHIANS I. 10.

Παρακαλω δε ὑμας, ἀδελφοι, δια τε ὀνομαῖος
τε Κυριε ἡμων Ἰησε Χριςε, ἱνα το αὑτο λε-
γηῖε πανῖες, και μη ἡ ἐν ὑμιν σχισμαῖα.

*Now I befeech you, brethren, by the name of
our Lord Jefus Chrift, that ye all fpeak the fame
thing, and that there be no divifions among
you.*

FROM thefe words of St. Paul, it is
evident, that many different opinions,
and many controverfies concerning them,
had found their way into the Chriftian
churches, at fo early a period as his life-
time. Thefe he endeavoured to fupprefs,
by thus enjoining them to fpeak the fame
things; that is, to fettle fome uniform rule
of faith and mode of worfhip, afcertained
by fomething like creeds or articles, to which
they could all affent; without which, no rule
of faith, or form of worfhip, could be eftablifhed, nor divifions amongft them be prevented,

vented, deſtructive to every community civil or religious. It is true, indeed, that at the firſt promulgation of the goſpel, Chriſt himſelf impoſed no ſuch on his diſciples, who chiefly conſiſted of the moſt ignorant and illiterate vulgar, from whom nothing more was required than the bare acknowledgment that he was the Son of God, or the Meſſiah, who had been long expected. As this is but a ſingle propoſition, no difference of opinion concerning it could ariſe amongſt thoſe who believed, and therefore there could be no occaſion for any teſts to reconcile them. In a little time the great, the wiſe, and the learned ſages and philoſophers became proſelytes, and brought with them a variety of opinions from their reſpective ſchools in which they had been educated; which were blended with the doctrines of Chriſt, and very ſoon corrupted the purity of his religion. It then became neceſſary to fix ſome ſtandard of truth, to which every Chriſtian might reſort; and when theſe doctrines were committed to writing,

ing, in the books of the New Testament, from the uncertainty of all human language, and the various interpretations which they will admit of, this necessity was greatly increased, and is daily increasing by time, which every day introduces new errors, and new disputes about them; so that it seems impossible, that, without some test, any religion can be established in any country; and without some establishment no national religion can subsist at all.

Hence appears the absurdity of those who would reject all religious tests, because Christ imposed none on his disciples when there were no errors to encounter nor controversies to decide, and therefore none were wanted: to reject them now, because they were then unnecessary, is as ridiculous as to explode the use of all medicines, because none were administered before any diseases had made their appearance. But, say some, If tests are necessary, let them be as comprehensive as possible; a declaration that we believe the scriptures, would be fully sufficient.

ficient. They ought, undoubtedly, to be as comprehenfive as the end of their inftitution will admit; which is, to exclude all thofe from a community, whofe principles muft induce them to betray and fubvert it : but fuch a declaration would, by no means, an-fwer this purpofe, becaufe our difputes are not about the truth, but the meaning, of thofe writings ; and we fee many who be-lieve, or pretend to believe, them, and yet deny their affent to every material doctrine which they contain, and juftify their diffent by their own interpretations : a teft, there-fore, muft fpecify and decide upon the par-ticular doctrines which are difputed, or it is entirely ufelefs and ineffectual. Such are the articles of our church, interpretations of the fenfe of the fcriptures, and explanations of the doctrines therein contained ; as fuch only we fubfcribe them, not as objects of our reafon or belief, any farther than we believe them to be fo. This, furely, is very different from afferting their truth in the firft in-ftance ; this depends on the veracity of the

books

books which they profess to explain; and
this on many other different considerations,
as the authenticity of those writings, the inspiration, and degrees of inspiration, of their
authors, and the purity of their preserva-
tion; with all which, in subscribing to these
articles, we have nothing to do. All that
is incumbent on us is, to compare them with
the books themselves, which, if we fairly
and candidly perform, I am persuaded, we
shall find them more consonant with their
real and genuine sense, and more expressive
of their true meaning, than modern theological language and ideas will admit of. The
compilers never considered whether they
are conformable to reason; if they expressed
the true sense of the scriptures, this was all
they intended.

1 Corin-

1 Corinthians I. 25.

Ὅτι τὸ μωρον τȣ Θεȣ, σοφωτερον των ἀνθρω-
πων ἐςι.

The foolishness of God is wiser than men.

THERE is something, at first sight, in this expression, indecent, if not impious; but it means no more than this; that the doctrines of Christianity, revealed by God, though they were "to the Jews a "stumbling-block, and to the Greeks foolish-"ness," are wiser (that is, better fitted to instruct mankind in the principles of true religion and sound morality) than all the theological lessons of the Rabbis of the one, or the Philosophers of the other. St. Paul, who says this, was, perhaps, as great a master of reason as any man of his own or of all succeeding ages; but he never employed it on subjects to which it cannot properly be applied: he never endeavours by it to explain the mysteries of the Christian religion,

or

or to reject them becaufe he is not able ; he believed them himfelf, and taught them to others, juft as they had been delivered by his Lord and mafter, without attempting to reconcile them to his own reafon, or that of his difciples.

Chrift frequently declared, that all mankind come into this world in a ftate of depravity, guilt, and condemnation ; that he was the Meffiah, or the Son of God, who came to inftruct and reform them, and to lay down his life as a propitiation for their tranfgreffions; and that his heavenly Father, on their fincere repentance, would accept his fufferings and death as an atonement for their fins : that they were free agents, and as fuch accountable for their conduct ; and yet conftantly afferts, that they can do nothing of themfelves, but that all their thoughts and actions muft proceed from the influence of God, " in " whom they live, and move, and have their " being." Thefe doctrines appeared to the learned philofophers of Rome and Athens

to

to be foolishness (that is, absurdities, contradictory to every principle of human reason) and so they must have done to St. Paul, had he brought them before the same tribunal; but he never presumed to set up human reason as a judge of divine dispensations. He pretended not to controvert the truth of these doctrines, by arguing, that it was never possible that a wise, benevolent, and just Creator should call into being creatures in a state of depravity, guilt, and condemnation, and punish them for what they could not prevent; nor that, if they could be criminal, he should accept the sufferings of the innocent as a satisfaction for the crimes of the guilty: nor did he alledge, that Omnipotence itself could not create beings at the same time free agents, yet under perpetual influence and direction: all these doubts and difficulties he left to the discussion of the reasoning divines and philosophers of later ages; for himself, he was satisfied of the truth of these doctrines, by the authority from whence they were derived;

rived; and as fuch, has tranfmitted them to us, in words as clear and explicit as the power of language can furnifh. He does not attempt to explain thefe myfteries, nor enters into any metaphyfical fpeculations on the abftract nature of guilt and punifhment, of fufferings or atonement, of free will, predeftination, and divine influence. He afferts the facts only as he received them; which is all of which, in our prefent ftate, we can be informed.

1 CORINTHIANS VII. 27.

Λελυσαι απο γυναικος; μη ζητει γυναικα.

Art thou loosed from a wife? seek not a wife.

ST. Paul, throughout this whole chapter, recommends celibacy to Christians of both sexes, as most acceptable to God, and most consistent with the purity of their religion. Commentators, I know, in order to extricate themselves from some difficulties, have represented this advice but as local and temporal, occasioned only by the distresses and persecutions under which the Christian churches at that time laboured: but, if we believe his own words, we must see that this was not his only, nor yet his principal reason for giving it; but that he meant it generally, because he was of opinion that marriage, in Christians of both sexes, multiplied their attachments, and increased their cares concerning worldly affairs, and consequently diverted their attention from the

sole

sole object of their profession, which is the attainment of everlasting life. He says, "I would have you without carefulness. He "that is unmarried careth for the things "which belong to the Lord; but he that "is married careth for the things of the "world, how he may please his wife.—The "unmarried woman careth for the things of "the Lord, that she may be holy both in "body and in spirit; but she that is married "careth for the things of the world, how she "may please her husband." For this reason, St. Paul here ventures to avow a doctrine contradictory to the moral and political sentiments of the wisest philosophers and legislators of all times, destructive of domestic happiness and national prosperity, and which, if universally adopted, would eradicate the human species from the face of the earth.

From hence, if we believe that this great Apostle understood the spirit of the religion which he taught, we cannot avoid drawing this conclusion—That there may be actions,

the

the performance of which may effentially contribute to raife individuals nearer to Chriftian perfection, and to qualify them for happinefs in a future life, which may yet widely differ, both in their principles and their end, from moral virtues, and which, if univerfally practifed, would be exceedingly detrimental to mankind in their prefent ftate.

Of thefe celibacy is one; which, though deftructive of the happinefs, and even of the exiftence of mankind, may yet give leifure to fome few individuals to carry their piety, devotion, virtue, and refignation, to a more exalted height than can be arrived at, under the many cares, connections, and embarraffments incident to the married ftate. In like manner, to fell all that a man hath, and give it to the poor, is an act which, if generally practifed, muft put an end to all trade, manufactures, and induftry, and introduce univerfal idlenefs and want; yet, the performance of it muft proceed from fo extraordinary a degree of faith, obedience, and

self-denial,

self-denial, that it may deserve, and receive, an extraordinary reward. Precepts of this sort, I apprehend, are not enjoined, but only occasionally flung out, to teach us the nature of Christian perfection; which is so adverse to the world, and all its œconomy, pursuits, and occupations, that we are neither required or expected to attain it in our present state, but ought to make as near approaches to it as our natural depravity and imperfection will permit.

From hence I am inclined to think, that, if monastic institutions were really what they pretend to be, voluntary retreats from all worldly cares, occupations, and connections, wholly appropriated to religious contemplation, piety, and devotion, they might confer very essential benefits on the very few individuals who are capable of receiving them, without any detriment to the business or population of the world. But the great objection to them is this—that they are not made for man, nor man for them. The generality of mankind are formed for

action,

action, and not for contemplation, and come into the world to do its bufinefs, without perceiving the folly and infignificance of what they are employed in. If multitudes, therefore, are confined in thefe gloomy manfions, in contradiction to their inclinations and dipofitions, they muft foon become, like other prifons, feminaries of ignorance, lazinefs, profligacy, and vice.

1 CORIN-

1 Corinthians XIII. 4, 5, 6, 7.

Ἡ ἀγαπη μακροθυμει, χρητευεται· ἡ
ἀγαπη ᾿ ζηλοι· ἡ ἀγαπη ᾿ περπερευεται, ᾿
φυσιεται,

᾿κ ἀσχημονει, ᾿ ζητει τα ἑαυτης, ᾿ παρ-
οξυνεῖαι, ᾿ λογιζεται το κακον,

᾿ χαιρει επι τη ἀδικιᾳ, συῖχαιρει δε τη
ἀληθειᾳ.

παντα τεγει, παντα πιτευει, παντα ἐλ-
πιζει, πανῖα ὑπομενει.

*Charity fuffereth long, and is kind; charity
envieth not; charity vaunteth not itself, is
not puffed up,*

*Doth not behave itfelf unfeemly, feeketh not
her own, is not eafily provoked, thinketh no
evil;*

*Rejoiceth not in iniquity, but rejoiceth in the
truth;*

*Beareth all things, believeth all things,
hopeth all things, endureth all things.*

IN this inimitable portrait of Charity,
drawn by the mafterly hand of St. Paul,

we

we find every virtue which conſtitutes the character of a Chriſtian, who is a candidate for the kingdom of heaven; in which it is remarkable, that there is not one, which is not peculiarly calculated to qualify men to become members, and to enjoy and contribute to the felicity, of that holy and happy ſociety.

"Charity ſuffereth long, and is kind;" that is, is patient, meek, and benevolent, qualities the moſt eſſential to ſocial happineſs. "Charity envieth not;" for, as the envious are miſerable, in proportion to the happineſs they ſee others enjoy, they would be more miſerable in heaven than they are upon earth. "Charity vaunteth not itſelf, "is not puffed up;" becauſe nothing ſo much diſturbs the peace of ſociety, as pride, inſolence, and ambition. "Doth not be- "have itſelf unſeemly;" that is, is not in converſation ill-bred, ſelf-ſufficient, diſputatious, and overbearing; offences, perhaps, more adverſe to ſocial happineſs, than many crimes of a more enormous kind. "Seeketh "not her own, is not eaſily provoked;" that is, is, rather chuses to give up some part of her property, to which she has an undoubted right, than be the cause of contests, animosities, and litigations, and is not easily provoked to enter into them, either by interests or resentment. " Thinketh no evil;" that is, suspects no evil intentions in the hearts of others, as she feels none in her own. " Rejoiceth not in iniquity, but rejoiceth in " the truth;" that is, takes no pleasure in any kind of wickedness, nor sees it with approbation in others ; but is happy in the practice of every virtue which is prescribed by reason and truth, and rejoiceth to see others follow her example. " Beareth all things," all injuries and insults, without anger, or a wish for revenge or retaliation. " Believeth all things," because meek, docile, diffident of her own judgment, and unsuspicious of fraud and imposition. " Hopeth all things," however unfavourable are their present appearances, will turn out for the best ; and therefore " endureth all things," pain, sickness, poverty, and misfortunes, with patience, and perfect resignation to the will of God.

We have here a compleat catalogue of all thofe virtues and difpofitions, which are neceffary to qualify a Chriftian for the kingdom of heaven; in any one of which, if he is deficient, he muft infallibly be excluded, however eminent his merits may be of another kind; of this the fame Apoftle affures us, who fays, "Though I fpeak with the "tongues of men and angels, and have not "charity, I am become as founding brafs, or "a tinkling cymbal; and though I have the "gift of prophecy, and underftand all myf- "teries, and all knowledge, and though I "have all faith, fo that I could remove "mountains, and have not charity, I am "nothing. And though I beftow all my "goods to feed the poor, and though I "give my body to be burned, and have not "charity, it profiteth me nothing;" that is, in regard to my attainment of the kingdom of heaven; becaufe there neither eloquence, nor prophecy, nor theological knowledge, nor faith, nor martyrdom, nor bounty to the poor, are wanted; but only fuch a

5   meek,

meek, humble, patient, peaceable, forgiving, and benevolent temper and behaviour, as is here ſpecified under the denomination of charity, which alone can enable us to communicate and participate happineſs, either in the preſent or a future ſtate.

1 CORIN-

1 CORINTHIANS XIII. 11.

Ὅτε ἤμην νηπιℚ, ὡς νηπιℚ ἐλαλℰν, ὡς νηπιℚ ἐφρονℰν, ὡς νηπιℚ ἐλοℊζομην· ὅτε δε γεγονα ἀνηρ, κατηργηκα τα τℰ νηπιℰ.

When I was a child, I spake as a child, I understood as a child, I thought as a child; but when I became a man, I put away childish things.

IF we trace a man through the different periods of his life, from the cradle to the grave, he appears in such a variety of shapes, that we can scarcely believe him to be the same creature. At first he is an helpless infant in his nurse's arms, without speech, understanding, or thought; then he is a child, speaking as a child, understanding as a child, thinking as a child. He is next a rude, unformed, impetuous school boy; and then transformed into a youth, graceful, amiable, and amorous. At length, arrived at compleat

pleat manhood, he puts away childiſh
things, and becomes a philoſopher, a war-
rior, or a ſtateſman. We then find him
meaſuring out the heavens, inveſtigating
other worlds, or buſied in the occupations
of this. We ſee him commanding fleets or
armies, or haranguing at the bar, in the
pulpit, or the ſenate; and at laſt return-
ing back to his primitive ſtate of child-
hood and imbecility. Yet, under all theſe
characters, he is but the ſame ſingle individual.

In what this identity conſiſts, or where
it reſides, it is by no means eaſy to aſ-
certain. It cannot be in the body, becauſe
every naturaliſt knows that the component
parts of the body are in perpetual motion,
are continually diſcharged by various eva-
cuations, and replaced by the particles of
our daily food; ſo that, in the courſe of
a few years, not a ſingle atom of our original frame can poſſibly remain. If a
man loſes a leg or an arm, or even both
legs

legs and arms, he is not lefs the fame
perfon; and therefore we have reafon to
conclude, that his identity would not be
affected by the lofs of his whole body; and
therefore in that it cannot refide.

It cannot be in the mind, becaufe the
changes of the mind are as great and
as frequent as thofe of the body, throughout the different ftages of human life;
the ideas of a man and thofe of a child
are as unlike as his features and his fta-
ture; at different ages we put away all
our former modes of thinking and acting,
and adopt new opinions, purfuits, inclinations, and attachments. Many difeafes
deftroy all our mental faculties, derange
our reafon, extinguifh our confcioufnefs,
and obliterate our memories; and yet our
identity remains unimpaired. If, therefore, it is not to be found either in the
body or the mind, there muft be fome
permanent principle in the human compofition, in which it does refide, totally
unaffected

unaffected by the continual alterations of them both;—and this, I think, is a new and unanswerable proof of the exiſtence and duration of the ſoul.

1 CORIN-

1 CORINTHIANS XIII. 12.

Βλεπομεν γαρ αρτι δι ἐσοπτρȣ ἐν αἰνιγματι.

For now we see through a glass, darkly.

SO darkly, indeed, do we see the things of a future life, and so erroneously those of the present, that we form very false estimates of them both; and act still more absurdly than we judge. There are, who not convinced that there will be a future state of retribution after death, and none who know not that the death of every man may be instantaneous, and cannot be far off; and yet they take no care to prepare themselves for the former, and think so little of the latter, that, on any unexpected event, it is become proverbial to say, I thought of it no more than of my dying day. We fear nothing so much as death ; and yet there is nothing which we think of so little. We are more tenacious of riches the less we want them, and toil away the best part of

our

our days to enable us to pass a few in a quiet leisure, which no man could ever enjoy who had ever been busy. We infuse into our children the same false ideas, and thus transmit absurdities from generation to generation. We educate them all for this life; there is not one school for the next. "What man is there of you," says Christ, "who, if his son ask for a fish, will give him "a serpent* ?" few, indeed, with regard to this world, are so foolish or so cruel, but, with regard to another, it is universally practised. Every prudent parent endeavours to infuse into his son the wisdom of the serpent, rather than the innocence of the fish. He spares no pains to qualify them for the highest posts in the kingdom of the earth, but his ambition extends not, like that of the mother of Zebedee, to gain them rank in the kingdom of heaven. Do we hear any father, however worthy and respectable, thus address his son, in the lan-

* Matt. vii. 10.

guage of a philosopher and a Christian?
I shall leave you, my son, an estate, small
indeed in the estimation of the world, but
sufficient to afford you, not only the neces-
saries but the comforts of life, and even to ad-
minister them to the wants of others : waste it
not in vice and extravagance, nor yet labour
to increase it by frauds and rapine, nor even
by honest industry in professions which will
not allow you leisure, either to enjoy this
life or prepare for another; but, above
all other methods, seek not to augment it
by a mercenary marriage, which cannot fail
to lead you into an inextricable labyrinth
of wickedness and misery ; and remember,
that mutual fidelity and affection will give
you more happiness than wealth is able to
bestow.

The very reverse of this is the lesson in-
culcated by every prudent parent, and ra-
tified by universal approbation.—My son,
he says, you will inherit an ample fortune;
but let not this tempt you to sit down quietly in an indolent insignificance : there are
a variety

a variety of methods by which you may improve it, and advance yourself in the world; by a difcreet marriage, you may double it, if you do not foolifhly facrifice your interefts; the law, the church, and the army are all open to your endeavours, and may reward them with the higheft pofts of honour and profit: the Eaft and the Weft are ftill unexhaufted, and ready to pour their treafures into the laps of the brave and enterprizing. By fuch inftructions are the feeds of avarice and ambition fown in the minds of youth, which afterwards infallibly produce the bitter fruits of iniquity and difappointment.

That mankind fhould thus continue, through all ages and generations, to think, fpeak, and act in contradiction to their reafon, their principles, and their intereft, is a wonderful phænomenon; which can be occafioned folely by this fingle circumftance, that they " fee through a glafs, " darkly:" whenever they fee clearly, they feldom judge wrong; the defect is not in

their

their reason, but in their knowledge; every one would pursue his own interest, if he knew what it was, and, in fact, every one does pursue it, but the generality totally mistake it. No man would choose riches before happiness, power before quiet, or fame before safety, if he knew the true value of each: no man would prefer the transitory and worthless enjoyment of this world to the permanent and sublime felicity of a better, if he had a clear prospect of them both; but we see the former through a mist, which always magnifies, and the latter appears to be at so great a distance, that we scarce see it at all; and therefore it makes little impression on our senses, and has as little influence on our conduct.

Why our all-wise and benevolent Creator should have thought proper thus to present all objects to our view, " through a glass, " darkly," is one of the many divine dispensations for which we are unable to account; but this we may know, that if we saw the things of this world clearly, and in

a true

a true light, the bufinefs and œconomy of it, conftituted as it is, could not go on ; our purfuits would all be at an end, when we faw there was nothing worth purfuing, our hopes would vanifh, our expectations be extinguifhed, and an univerfal ftagnation would enfue : and from hence we have reafon to conclude, that a diftinct profpect of the things of another world, while we refide in this, would be equally detrimental to the well being of both.

PHILIP-

PHILIPPIANS IV. 8.

Το λοιπον, αδελφοι, ὁσα ἐςιν αληθη, ὁσα
σεμνα, ὁσα δικαια, ὁσα αγνα, ὁσα προσφιλη,
ὁσα ευφημα, εἰ τις αρετη και εἰ τις ἐπαιν©,
ταυτα λογιζεσθε.

*Finally, brethren, whatsoever things are
true, whatsoever things are honest, whatsoever
things are just, whatsoever things are pure,
whatsoever things are lovely, whatsoever
things are of good report; if there be any virtue, and if there be any praise, think on these
things.*

I T is not, I think, a little surprizing to
see many Christian divines, of the first
learning and abilities, employing that learning and those abilities, and much of their
time, in framing laborious systems of ethics
from the law of nature, whilst they have
the books of the New Testament continually lying open before their eyes. In Plato
and Aristotle, in Cicero and Seneca, this
was a laudable and useful undertaking; but,

in

in a Chriſtian, it is neither uſeful or meritorious, nor wiſer than if any one ſhould
chuſe to ſhut his eyes in the brighteſt day-
light, only to try if he was able to grope
out his way in the dark. It is now as
impoſſible for any man to form a religious and moral inſtitution by the mere
efforts of human reaſon, as to ſee by a
farthing candle in the midſt of a meridian
ſunſhine. He muſt unavoidably adopt the
doctrines and precepts of the Goſpel, and
then miſtake them for his own. If his own
are true and juſt, they muſt be exactly the
ſame; and if they differ, they are unworthy of notice. If we believe the doctrine and precepts tranſmitted to us in the
New Teſtament to be a revelation from
God, we cannot, without preſumption,
ſearch out for any other, nor even accept
the ſame on an inferior authority. Whatever may be their authority, their unrivalled
excellence is indiſputable. The moral leſ-
ſons of Chriſt are all ſo conciſe, ſo clear, ſo
perſuaſive, ſo unencumbered with definitions

and

and inquiries, and enforced by parables so apposite and instructive, as brings them nearer to our hearts, and renders them not only superior to, but unlike all which had ever before been published to the world. In omitting all unnecessary disquisitions on moral and religious subjects, the Apostles imatated the example of their master. In the passage now before us, St. Paul, writing to the brethren at Philippi, enjoins them to think on, that is, not to forget to practise, " whatsoever things are true, whatso-" ever things are honest, whatsoever things " are just, whatsoever things are pure." He takes it for granted, that those to whom he wrote, as well as all mankind, knew what things are true, honest, just, and pure ; and therefore he enters not into any metaphysical inquiries into the abstract nature of truth, honesty, justice, and purity, which are always useless, and sometimes detrimental, as they never induce men to be virtuous, and sometimes serve to furnish them with excuses for vices. Men want not knowledge

ledge of their duty, but inclination to perform it. A definition of virtue will never
make any one leſs profligate, nor an enquiry concerning the origin of property
make any one more honeſt; no more
than a diſſertation on optics will make a
man ſee, or a receipt for diſtilling brandy
or brewing ſtrong beer will make him
ſober.

2 THESSALONIANS II. 11.

Και δια τυτο πεμψει αυτοις ο Θεος ενεργειαν
πλανης, εις το πιϛευσαι αυτυς τω ψευδει.

*And for this caufe God fhall fend them ftrong
delufion, that they fhould believe a lie.*

IN this, and feveral other places in both
the Old and New Teftament, God is
reprefented as leading men into errors deftructive to their innocence and happinefs,
fometimes by his own, and fometimes by
the influence of intermediate fpirits. How
is this reconcileable with his juftice and
goodnefs? How can any evil proceed from
infinite goodnefs, or any delufion from the
fountain of all truth? No commentator or
preacher on thefe texts, that I know of,
has yet been able to anfwer thefe queftions in a manner fatisfactory to reafon or
common fenfe

But this difficulty, like moft others in our
interpretations of fcripture, arifes from our

5   own

own ignorance and our infenſibility of it. We boldly and preſumptuouſly aſſert, that God cannot do one thing, and that he will not do another, becauſe ſuch things ſeem to us to be inconſiſtent with thoſe attributes which we have thought proper , to beſtow upon him ; but we know ſo little of the nature of good and evil, of truth or falſhood, of God or man, or of the relations between a Creator and his creatures, that we are utterly incapable to preſcribe limits to his power, or rules to his will ; as well might a worm pretend to decide on the councils of princes, and the policies of empires, as man to paſs judgment on the diſpenſations of the Almighty. We ſay, God cannot be the cauſe of any evil ; but we know not what is evil ; he may be, and is, the cauſe of many things which appear, and really are, evils to us, however they may be neceſſary to the production of univerſal good. We ſay, he cannot be the cauſe of any deluſion ; but why not ? truth is by no means the criterion of virtue, as

                                    ſome

some philosophers would persuade us; delusion, in itself, is neither good or evil; its merit or criminality depends on the end for which it is intended: it is no crime to deceive men for their entertainment, much less for their benefit; there is no immorality in writing a play, a poem, or romance, because it is fiction, but great merit, if it is calculated to promote virtue, or to discourage vice. The whole of this life is a succession of delusions, kindly imposed upon us by our Creator, to enable us to support the sufferings, and carry on the business of it. The fallacy of each we discover in its turn, but never till it has attained its end. It is all mere scenery, a beautiful illusion, in which every object, being placed at a proper distance, and seen through a false medium, appears as it ought, but never as it is. Wealth, honours, and pleasures, are exhibited in the clearest light, to incite our industry; but the vanity of their possessions is hid for a time under a cloud, that we may not sink

into

into sloth and inactivity. Thus we may be said to believe a lie, that is, what is not true; unexperienced, we believe that the prosperity of this world will make us compleatly happy, that the period of life is of long duration, and that the hour of death is ever at a great distance; in every one of which we find ourselves constantly deceived; on which beneficent deception all our enjoyments, hopes, expectations, and pursuits intirely depend. If God, therefore, by means of these kind delusions, dispenses undeserved blessings on mankind, why may he not sometimes inflict such punishments upon them, as their offences may have deserved, by the same means, either by his own power, or the operations of intermediate spirits? We know that he has given us power to deceive and ensnare, as well as to destroy, inferior animals; a power which we daily exercise without scruple, without arraigning his justice or our own. Why then may he not, with equal justice, grant the

same

same power over us, to beings of superior orders?

We may further add, that there are many passages, in both the Old and New Testament, similar to this before us, which are, in fact, nothing more than modes of expression usually made use of by the writers of those books, who generally impute every event and action, whether good or evil, just or unjust, to God himself, without any reference to second causes. Every disposition of men's hearts, and every act proceeding from them, are ascribed immediately to God; by which nothing more is to be understood, than that such were men's hearts, and such things were done. This, in a large and extensive view, is certainly right, because the great Creator and disposer of all things must primarily be the cause of all dispositions, actions, and events; because the First Cause must be the cause of every cause from whence they can proceed: but how this is consistent with that

freewill,

freewill, of which we know and feel we ourselves are poffeffed, is far above the reach of our imperfect comprehenfions; reafon affures us that both are true, and fcripture every where confirms this conclufion.

J A M E S

JAMES IV. 1.

Ποθεν πολεμοι και μαχαι εν υμιν; εκ
εν]ευθεν, εκ των ηδονων υμων των ςρατευομενων
εν τοις μελεσιν υμων;

*From whence come wars and fighting among
you? come they not hence, even of your lusts?*

AS war and peace so essentially affect
the morals, as well as the happiness
of mankind, it seems extraordinary that the
great Author of the Christian religion should
have given no directions on so important
a subject. The Apostle here decides nothing concerning the lawfulness of wars
amongst Christians, but only informs us
from whence they proceed, which is from
their ungoverned passions, anger and revenge, avarice and ambition; nor do we
find, in any part of the New Testament, that
they are either absolutely allowed or positive-
ly forbid. This remarkable silence, I think,
is not difficult to be accounted for; because,

if

if Chriſt had encouraged, or even expreſsly permitted, his diſciples to carry on wars and fightings, he would have given the ſanction of divine authority to all the wickedneſs and miſery, which inevitably attend them ; and if he had abſolutely forbid them to fight on any occaſion, he muſt have left every country, in which his religion ſhould prevail, a defenceleſs prey to every infidel invader ; he prudently, therefore, rather choſe to leave their defence to the operations of their own paſſions and vices, which he knew, notwithſtanding all his pacific precepts, would always be ſufficient for that purpoſe.—But although in this, as well as in many other inſtances, Providence employs the iniquities of men to bring about beneficial ends, this leſſens not their criminality, or juſtifies thoſe who commit them. All the precepts of Chriſt, and every principle of the religion which he taught, are diametrically oppoſite to thoſe of war : theſe require a poor, meek, and humble ſpirit ; which thoſe repreſent as infamous and contemptible: thefe exhort us to live peaceably with all men; which is certainly incompatible with a ftate of war: thefe recommend patience and forbearance under the greateft infults; thofe the quickeft and moft violent refentment: thefe enjoin us to love and ferve our enemies; thofe to deftroy them with fire and fword. How at the fame time we can ferve thefe two mafters, or how their commands can be made confiftent with each other, I muft leave to fome pious and valiant Chriftian hero to explain.

F I N I S.